Editor
Tom Finley

Assistant Editor
Lauren Ajer

Consulting Editors
Rick Bundschuh
Kathi Mills
Annette Parrish

Contributing Writers
Carol Bostrom
Ed Reed
Bobbie Reed

Designed and Illustrated by Tom Finley

The standard Bible text used in this course is the Holy Bible, *The New International Version.* Copyright © 1973, 1978, 1984 by the International Bible Society. Used by permission of Zondervan Bible Publishers.

Also used is: *NASB—The New American Standard Bible* © The Lockman Foundation 1960, 1962, 1963, 1968, 1971, 1972, 1973, 1975. Used by permission.

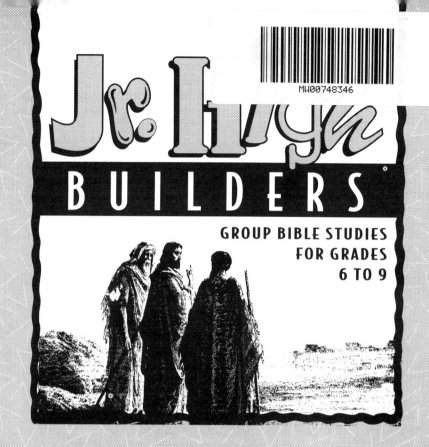

Jr. High BUILDERS

GROUP BIBLE STUDIES
FOR GRADES
6 TO 9

THE CHRISTIAN BASICS

NUMBER 1 IN A SERIES OF 12

Gospel Light

INTRODUCTION: OVERVIEW OF THE PARTS AND PIECES

This book contains everything you need to teach any size group of junior high students about the basics of Christianity. Thirteen sessions, with complete session plans for the leader, reproducible classroom worksheets and reproducible take-home sheets. Also, thirteen lecture-oriented Bible study outlines based on the same themes, to provide your students with needed reinforcement from a fresh perspective. And—dozens of action games and a section of clip art featuring illustrations to promote your Bible studies and dress up your announcement handbills.

Contents

The Parts and Pieces

● The **SESSION PLAN** contains two essential ingredients for a meaningful Bible study all students will enjoy: a commentary section to provide the leader with important biblical information and to set the stage for the lesson; and a lesson plan filled with Bible learning activities to help students retain spiritual truths. **FOR A DETAILED DESCRIPTION, TURN TO PAGE 4.**

Belief

SESSION 1

INSIGHTS FOR THE LEADER

WHAT THE SESSION IS ABOUT
True belief means forming a personal relationship with Christ.

SCRIPTURE STUDIED
John 1:12; 3:16; 6:40,47; 11:25,27; Acts 16:30,34.

KEY PASSAGE
"For God so loved the world that he gave his one and only Son, that whoever believes in him should not perish but have eternal life."
John 3:16

AIMS OF THE SESSION
During this session your learners will:

1. Underst—

We begin our examination of the fundamentals of Christian living with a look at **belief.**

Young people often can talk about the Christian faith and quote or refer to Scripture without fully understanding the meaning behind the words and phrases they are using. This session will get your class off to a good start by giving learners the opportunity to clarify their understanding of what it means to believe in Jesus.

As you prepare to guide your students through this learning experience, use the information in this Bible Study section for your study. Then you will be prepared to answer questions or clarify concepts as the lesson proceeds.

What Is Belief?
It is important to understand the meaning of belief. It is more than knowing facts about Jesus. Believing means —

Christ. Some people can identify the moment when they decided to begin that relationship. Others, particularly those who grew up in Christian homes, cannot name the moment the decision was made, but they know that they are now in a relationship with Christ and that they have been born again. Each person is individually responsible for a decision to believe in Christ or to reject Him. Having Christian parents or going to church cannot automatically make one a Christian: only a deliberate choice to receive Christ can do that.

Belief Leads to Salvation
When we do believe in Jesus, we are saved from perishing and we receive eternal life (see John 3:16,36; 6:40,47; 11:25-27). Jesus said, "For my Father's will is that everyone who looks to the Son and believes in him shall have eternal life, and I will raise him up at the last day

The **STUDENT WORKSHEET,** called the **Treasure Seeker,** allows the student to learn by doing rather than just sitting and listening. Photocopy as many sheets as you need. **SEE PAGE 6 FOR COMPLETE DETAILS.**

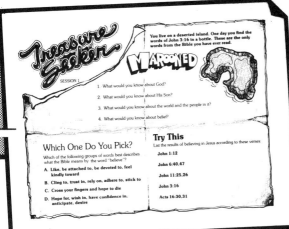

The **TEACHING RESOURCE PAGE** provides necessary items such as short stories or case studies when required by the **Session Plan.** Most **Session Plans** have no **Teaching Resource Page.** **FOR DETAILS, SEE PAGE 7.**

The **TAKE-HOME PAPER,** called the **Fun Page,** features a Bible game (such as a maze or crossword), and daily devotional questions and a memory verse for motivated students. **FOR MORE ABOUT THE FUN PAGE, TURN TO PAGE 8.**

The **POPSHEET** is a lecture-oriented version of the **Session Plan,** based on a different portion of the Scriptures. Use it as an alternative to the **Session Plan,** at another meeting later in the week, or combine it with the **Session Plan** as you see fit.

The **Popsheet** features **GAMES AND THINGS,** dozens of action games for your students to enjoy. **PAGE 10 CONTAINS DETAILS.**

The **CLIP ART AND OTHER GOODIES** section at the back of the book contains art and special charts you can use to promote your studies. **SEE PAGE 12 FOR COMPLETE INFORMATION.**

3

THE SESSION PLANS

How to squeeze the most out of each Bible study.

● **Every Session Plan contains the following features:**

1. INTRODUCTORY INFORMATION

WHAT THE SESSION IS ABOUT states the main thrust of the lesson.

Your students will examine all verses listed in **SCRIPTURE STUDIED.**

The **KEY PASSAGE** is also the memory verse given on the **Fun Page** take-home paper.

AIMS OF THE SESSION is what you hope to achieve during class time. You may wish to privately review these after class as a measure of your success.

Prayer

SESSION 7

WHAT THE SESSION IS ABOUT
Why, where, and when we should pray, and with what attitude.

SCRIPTURE STUDIED
Psalm 5:3; 86:6,7; Matthew 7:7,8; 21:22; Luke 5:16; 18:11-14; Romans 12:3; Hebrews 4:16.

KEY PASSAGE
"Pray continually."
1 Thessalonians 5:17

AIMS OF THE SESSION
During this session your learners will:
1. Discuss why, where, when and with what attitude to pray.
2. Describe ways each element of prayer may be applied to their daily life.
3. Select one thing to pray for.

INSIGHTS FOR THE LEADER

Young people often avoid prayer because they have found lengthy prayer times boring. Sometimes they are not sure about the right time and place for prayer. They may think Christians can pray only in a church. They may think you have to say a perfect prayer, with a lot of complicated words, like missionaries they have heard. They don't think God would be interested in what's happening in the life of a junior high. In addition to these misconceptions, they find it hard to concentrate. Their minds wander. It seems like more trouble than it's worth.

This session is designed to be an antidote to these problems. It demonstrates that prayer can happen anywhere. It shows junior highers that God wants to hear what is important to them. It deals with minds wandering during prayer times and with combating boredom.

Your lesson deals with the following questions: 1. Why pray? 2. Where can we pray? 3. When pray? 4. What...

Why should...
The reason... begin with 1... confess our si... This course h... forgiveness in...

tians sin they need God's forgiveness and cleansing. Then the burden of the sin is lifted and the person can continue to enjoy God's fellowship and keep on serving Him.

...other reason for prayer is, "Ask and it will be given to you; seek and you will find; knock and the door will be opened to you. For everyone who asks receives; he who seeks finds; and to him who knocks, the door will be opened" (Matt. 7:7,8). In this Ser...

2. INSIGHTS FOR THE LEADER

This part of each lesson is background for you, the leader. Study this section with your Bible open and watch for useful information and insights which will further equip you to lead the class session.

=●=**Three things to note about the Session Plan:**=

One, the **Session Plan** makes heavy use of **Bible learning activities** (BLA's). A Bible learning activity is precisely what it sounds like—an activity students perform to learn about the Bible. Because *action* is employed, the student has a much greater chance of **COMPREHENDING** and **RETAINING** spiritual insights. And because you the leader can see what the student is doing you can readily **MEASURE** the student's comprehension. The BLA allows you to **WALK AROUND THE CLASSROOM** as students work, answering questions or dealing with problem students. Furthermore, it's **EASIER TO TEACH WELL** using BLA's. If you've never used BLA's before, you will quickly find them much simpler to prepare and deliver than a whole session of lecture.

Two, the **Session Plan** provides guided conversation—suggestions on what to say throughout the class time. Notice that the guided conversation is always printed in **BOLD TYPE** in the **Session Plan.** LIGHT TYPE indicates instructions to you, the teacher.

Three, if special or unusual preparation is required before class begins, it will be listed immediately below the title **SESSION PLAN,** under the heading *BEFORE CLASS BEGINS.*

3. SESSION PLAN

This heading introduces the step-by-step lesson plan. With careful planning, you can easily tailor each session to the amount of class time you have.

4. ATTENTION GRABBER

Who knows what lurks in the minds of your students as they file into your room? The **Attention Grabber** will stimulate their interest and focus their thinking on the theme of the lesson.

The **Attention Grabber,** as well as other parts of the **Session Plan,** often—but not always—contain an additional alternate activity. These alternates are identified by the titles **"CREATIVE OPTION," "OPTIONAL"** or similar designations. Choose the activity that best suits the needs of your class and fits your time schedule.

5. BIBLE EXPLORATION

The **Bible Exploration** is the heart of your class session because it involves each learner directly in the study of God's Word. It is during this period that you will invite the students to explore and discover **WHAT THE BIBLE SAYS AND MEANS** and to discuss **HOW IT APPLIES TO EACH STUDENT.**

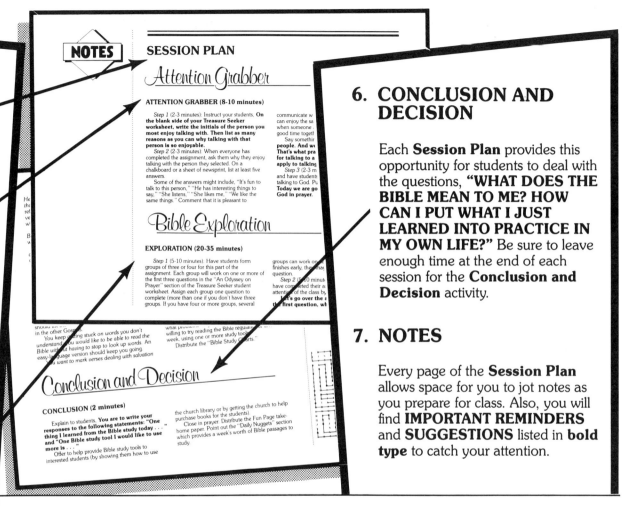

6. CONCLUSION AND DECISION

Each **Session Plan** provides this opportunity for students to deal with the questions, **"WHAT DOES THE BIBLE MEAN TO ME? HOW CAN I PUT WHAT I JUST LEARNED INTO PRACTICE IN MY OWN LIFE?"** Be sure to leave enough time at the end of each session for the **Conclusion and Decision** activity.

7. NOTES

Every page of the **Session Plan** allows space for you to jot notes as you prepare for class. Also, you will find **IMPORTANT REMINDERS** and **SUGGESTIONS** listed in **bold type** to catch your attention.

● Necessary Classroom Supplies

The Session Plan Bible study activities require that you make the following items readily available to students:

- A Bible for each student (Essential!) ● Paper and pencils or pens ● Scissors
- Felt markers ● Butcher paper for posters ● Transparent tape

You, the teacher, will need a chalkboard or overhead projector.

Special requirements will be listed in the NOTES section of the proper Session Plans.

5

THE TREASURE SEEKER STUDENT WORKSHEETS

The **Treasure Seeker** helps students dig out the treasure in God's Word for themselves.

The page immediately following each **Session Plan** is the **Treasure Seeker** worksheet for your students. Here's how to use them, in 5 easy steps:

You live on a deserted island. One day you find the words of John 3:16 in a bottle. These are the only words from the Bible you have ever read.

MAROONED

SESSION 1

1. What would you know about God?

2. What would you know about His Son?

● TRY THESE SPECIAL TIPS:

Photocopy all youth group announcements on the reverse side of the **Treasure Seeker**. The **Clip Art and Other Goodies** section at the back of this book will be a big help here.

Use different colored paper from week to week in your copier. If your machine can enlarge, print the worksheets "giant size" once in awhile.

Too much of even a good thing is too much. We suggest that every now and then you hand out blank paper and simply *read* the **Treasure Seeker** instructions to your students. Or write the instructions on the chalkboard. Or hand write and copy your own worksheets. Variety is the key.

1. Before class, use your church photocopier to reproduce enough student worksheets for your learners and a few extra for visitors. With rare exception, there is only one **Treasure Seeker** sheet per session. (You may wish to photocopy all 13 sessions at one time to save trips.)

2. The **Treasure Seekers** are generally used throughout each **Session Plan**. The best time to distribute them to students is when the **Session Plan** first calls for their use. Always keep a copy for yourself.

3. Be sure to have **plenty of blank paper** for students' written assignments—the **Treasure Seekers** don't have much extra space.

4. It may help to have your students fold their **Treasure Seeker** into their Bibles if there is a gap between uses of the worksheet. This will aid you in avoiding the Paper Airplane Syndrome.

5. Collect and save the worksheets at the end of each class. (Do not collect worksheets that contain private confessions to God or the like.) You can follow the progress of your students by examining their work. Parents, too, will want to see what their children are learning.

THE TEACHING RESOURCE PAGES

Special "goodies" to help you teach.

A few sessions require extra "goodies" such as board games or short stories. These are provided by the **Teaching Resource Pages** which follow the **Treasure Seeker** in the appropriate sessions.

The **Session Plans** and the **Resource Pages** contain complete instructions.

Teaching Resource
Benefit Puzzle

Cut out these pictures. Shuffle them and hand them out one card per person as students arrive at class. If necessary, photocopy this page so that there are enough pictures for your class. See the session's Attention Grabber activity for further instructions.

THE FUN PAGE TAKE-HOME PAPERS

Give your students a treat! The **Fun Page** combines games, memory verses and daily devotional studies into an enjoyable, fun-filled take-home paper.

Features:

Each **Fun Page** contains a Bible game designed to amplify the insights gained in the classroom. Mazes, crosswords, word searches—games ranging from the simple to the extremely challenging.

There's cartoon artwork, informal readability, and humor that your students will welcome.

The **Daily Nuggets** section is a simple six-day devotional based on passages related to the Scriptures studied in class. See "TIPS" for important advice.

The **Hot Thot** memory verse helps students lock the wisdom of God's Word into their minds and hearts.

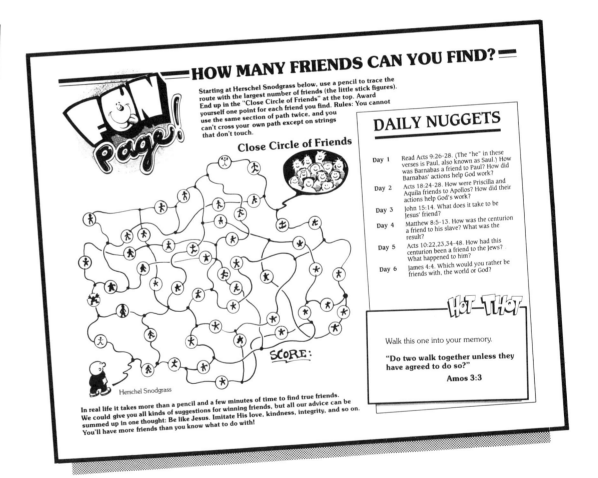

UH, OH! WE BROKE IT!

Why did God cause the Bible to be written to us? Good question! And the answer is in this word/picture game. Just one problem: we broke it. The first part is OK, but it is up to you to fix the rest of the game by placing the pictures at the bottom into the proper spaces in the game. Don't get the wrong combination or who knows what weird answer you'll find! This is a very tough game, so be patient. The solution is printed upside down at the bottom of the page.

– ter

DAILY NUGGETS

TIPS:

You can use the Fun Page several ways:

- As a **take-home paper** to extend the classroom into the week. Hand out copies as students leave class.
- As a special **Bible learning activity** during class. (Some of the games would make interesting **Attention Grabbers,** for example.)
- Make it the **focal point of another Bible study.** For instance, if you used the **Session Plan** Sunday morning, you could reinforce the lesson during an informal midweek meeting by involving students in answering the questions in the **Daily Nuggets** section.
- Even absentees can be involved. Put the **Fun Page** into an envelope along with a personal note to that learner who needs a little encouragement.

A word about MOTIVATION:

You won't have any trouble getting your students to play the games on the **Fun Page.** (Just see how many of them are playing the games during church service!) But the **Daily Nuggets** and the **Hot Thot** memory verse can be problems. Here are two ways to motivate students to answer the daily devotional questions and memorize the verse:

1. Start a contest. Award points to those students who complete the assignments, bring friends, and memorize passages. Pick a nice prize such as a free trip to camp and run the contest for about five weeks. (Longer makes for lack of interest.)

2. Combine the assignments with a discipleship class. If you are not personally involved in the discipleship program, give a copy of the **Fun Page** to the leader.

THE POPSHEET LECTURE BIBLE STUDIES

"Pop" these **Popsheets** out of this book and give them to the leader of your youth group's other meetings. Great for an at-home Bible study, a camp retreat, games night or special event.

Youth groups come in all sizes and shapes. So do youth programs. Meetings vary widely in style—ranging from Sunday morning Bible studies with singing and announcements, to deeper discipleship programs for motivated students, to the fun and action of "game nights" with very short Bible messages.

The **Popsheets** offer a good source of creative thinking for whatever type of program you have. **Popsheets** are packed with Bible stories, object lessons, case studies, discussion questions, and fast-paced games aimed at the junior high "squirrel" mentality! Each **Popsheet** covers the same theme as the accompanying **Session Plan,** but the stories, verses, object lessons and case studies are all new and fresh. The advantages?

- For students who attended the **Session Plan** class, a fresh new perspective on the topic. A great way to insure retention.

- For learners who missed the **Session Plan** class, a good way to keep current with the other students. This is a sound method to guarantee that all your youth group members explore every topic in a Bible study series.

- Or use your creativity to replace some of the Bible learning activities in the **Session Plan** with the **Popsheets'** object lessons and short stories.

THEME

The same theme as the accompanying **Session Plan**

BIBLE STUDY OUTLINE

A suggested Bible passage with a list of important points to make during your lecture. The **Bible Study Outline** offers a **basic** lesson plan to stimulate your thinking as you prayerfully prepare your message. **Use your own creativity and ability to "flesh it out."** There is plenty here for outstanding Bible messages your students will enjoy and remember.

Notice that the **Bible Study Outline** contains no **Bible learning activities.** The **Popsheet** is designed to be a short Bible message that you can give at an informal "games night," camp cabin devotional, or what have you.

OBJECT LESSON

Each **Popsheet** has an object lesson, short story, or case study. (A case study is a description of an event or situation a junior high student is likely to face in life.) These add spice to your messages. A good object lesson, for instance, and the spiritual truth it conveys, can be remembered for a lifetime.

DISCUSSION QUESTIONS

You may wish to involve your students in your lectures by asking them about the issues and implications of the Bible study. Feel free to modify or add to the questions to more nearly suit your students' needs.

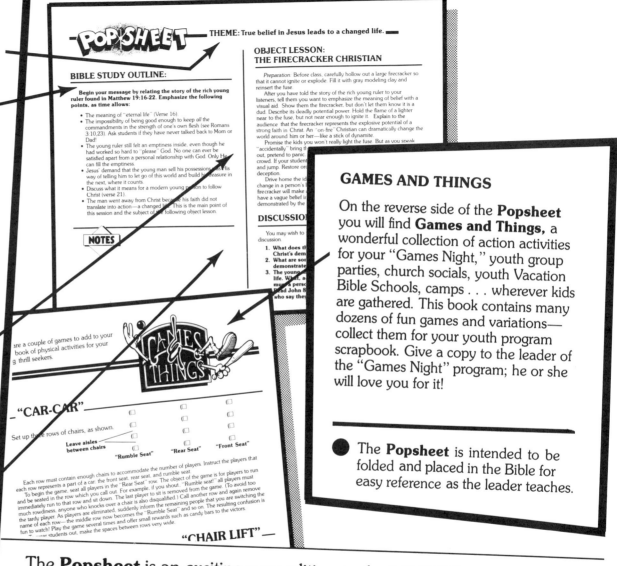

GAMES AND THINGS

On the reverse side of the **Popsheet** you will find **Games and Things,** a wonderful collection of action activities for your "Games Night," youth group parties, church socials, youth Vacation Bible Schools, camps . . . wherever kids are gathered. This book contains many dozens of fun games and variations—collect them for your youth program scrapbook. Give a copy to the leader of the "Games Night" program; he or she will love you for it!

● The **Popsheet** is intended to be folded and placed in the Bible for easy reference as the leader teaches.

The **Popsheet** is an exciting new edition to the **LIGHT FORCE** line of junior high Bible study materials. It contains truly useful features that will help make your informal Bible study meetings of keen interest to your learners.

The **Popsheet** is for you to use. Take advantage of it. Use it as an aid to your Bible study preparation and game plans. You'll be glad you did.

INTRODUCTION TO CLIP ART

Good news for those who can't draw.

If you want your class or youth group to increase in size—and who doesn't—you'll welcome the **Clip Art and Other Goodies** section found at the rear of this book. Create your own terrific monthly youth group activity calendars, announcement sheets and posters. It's fun and easy! Simply follow the tips and techniques in the Clip Art and Other Goodies section; you'll produce great "promo pieces" that will attract kids to your Bible studies and other events.

Remember: Even if you can't draw cartoons, with the right promotional clip art you can draw kids.

Belief

WHAT THE SESSION IS ABOUT

True belief means forming a personal relationship with Christ.

SCRIPTURE STUDIED

John 1:12; 3:16; 6:40,47; 11:25,27; Acts 16:30,34.

KEY PASSAGE

"For God so loved the world that he gave his one and only Son, that whoever believes in him should not perish but have eternal life."

John 3:16

AIMS OF THE SESSION

During this session your learners will:

1. Understand the Bible teaching that belief in Jesus Christ is the way to become a Christian.
2. Discuss what it means to believe in Jesus.
3. Select the most personally meaningful part of John 3:16.

INSIGHTS FOR THE LEADER

We begin our examination of the fundamentals of Christian living with a look at **belief.**

Young people often can talk about the Christian faith and quote or refer to Scripture without fully understanding the meaning behind the words and phrases they are using. This session will get your class off to a good start by giving learners the opportunity to clarify their understanding of what it means to believe in Jesus.

As you prepare to guide your students through this learning experience, use the information in this INSIGHTS FOR THE LEADER section for your study. Then you will be prepared to answer questions or clarify concepts as the lesson proceeds.

What Is Belief?

It is important to understand the meaning of belief. It is more than knowing facts about Jesus. **Believing means forming a relationship with Him and trusting Him enough to obey Him.** It is more than just a mental attitude. Faith requires action. You may have faith that a certain chair will hold you safely; but the chair does you no good, and your belief does you no good, unless you actually sit in the chair. Even so, a mental attitude of belief in Jesus is not the final step. You must take action that reflects your belief; you must begin a personal daily relationship with Jesus

Christ. Some people can identify the moment when they decided to begin that relationship. Others, particularly those who grew up in Christian homes, cannot name the moment the decision was made, but they know that they are now in a relationship with Christ and that they have been born again. Each person is individually responsible for a decision to believe in Christ or to reject Him. Having Christian parents or going to church cannot automatically make one a Christian: only a deliberate choice to receive Christ can do that.

Belief Leads to Salvation

When we do believe in Jesus, we are saved from perishing and we receive eternal life (see John 3:16,36; 6:40,47; 11:25-27). Jesus said, "For my Father's will is that everyone who looks to the Son and believes in him shall have eternal life, and I will raise him up at the last day . . . . I tell you the truth, he who believes has everlasting life" (John 6:40,47). Before raising Lazarus from the dead, Jesus said to Martha, "I am the resurrection and the life. He who believes in me will live, even though he dies; and whoever lives and believes in me will never die" (John 11:25,26). Belief is the way one receives the everlasting life that God offers through Jesus. When the Philippian jailer asked Paul and Silas, "What must I do to be saved?" they answered, "Believe in the Lord Jesus, and you will be saved" (Acts 16:30,31).

NOTES

It's as simple (**and as profound**) as that. Just believe, and you will be **saved**.

Other Scriptures tell of additional results of believing in Jesus. John 1:12 points out that those who believe in Jesus have the power, or the right, to become children of God, members of God's family. John 7:38 explains that belief in Jesus and the fullness of the Spirit result in "living water" flowing from within—a figurative way of speaking of the wonderful life God gives us. John 7:39 discusses belief as the means for receiving the Holy Spirit.

Christians use a number of terms to refer to the same experience; we may talk about being saved, becoming a Christian, believing in Christ, becoming members of God's family. Whatever expression we use, belief in Jesus is the basic ingredient.

Belief Has Risks

Students will find that faith has risks, costs, and results. They risk facing ridicule or persecution for their faith. The cost is the surrender of their wills to Jesus Christ, and then giving of their time and energy and resources to Him. The results are everlasting life, freedom from the guilt and penalty of sin, and a family relationship with the God of the universe.

SESSION PLAN

BEFORE CLASS BEGINS: If you intend to use the "CREATIVE OPTION" for the ATTENTION GRABBER, you'll need a baby rattle and a toy snake.

Attention Grabber

ATTENTION GRABBER (5 minutes)

On your chalkboard or overhead projector write these headings: "SANTA," "EASTER BUNNY," "TOOTH FAIRY," and "THE STORK." As students arrive, ask each to indicate which myth or myths he or she once believed. Place a check under each heading so indicated. ("THE STORK" refers to babies being brought to their parents by bird power.)

When everyone has responded—including you—ask students to describe some of the silly things they believed about these myths. After the class has had a good laugh, explain that this session focuses on belief in Christ. Be prepared to explain why belief in Jesus is different than the false beliefs young people once held. You might want to say something like this: **In childhood we had a lot of funny ideas, and sometimes we really believed them. Even though some people would say that believing in Christ is the same** as believing in our funny childhood ideas, there is a difference between believing the truth and believing a fantasy. Jesus is not made-up. He is the truth. He is real. And so our belief in Him is founded in reality and not in make-believe.

CREATIVE OPTION (10 minutes)

Materials needed: Baby rattle tied to a toy snake. A paper grocery bag to hold the "rattlesnake."

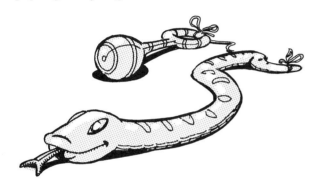

When students have arrived, hold up the sack for all to see. Say, **This bag contains a small rattlesnake. Raise your hand if you don't believe me.** When students raise hands, say, **I am not lying. This really is a rattlesnake in here. But keep your hands up if you still don't believe me.** Pick a disbelieving student and challenge him or her to come forward and place a hand in the bag.

Have the student reach in and hold up the snake. Offer congratulations for that person's courage of convictions. Say something like, **John did not believe I had a rattlesnake in here, and he was willing to place his hand in the bag to back up his conviction.** If no student will reach into the sack, hold up the snake and say, **Some of you *said* you didn't believe, yet you didn't have the courage to stand up for your convictions.**

Make a transition to the Bible Exploration by telling students that true belief is proved by *action*. **If you truly believed there was a real rattlesnake in the bag, you would be a fool to put your hand in there. If you believed there wasn't, you could prove that by putting your hand in. If you cannot back your belief by action, your belief isn't real. Today we are going to talk about the kind of belief it takes to become a Christian: belief that proves itself by action. The action that a person must take when he or she believes in Jesus is to form a personal relationship with Him.**

Bible Exploration

EXPLORATION (20-25 minutes)

Step 1 (5-10 minutes): Have students form discussion teams of two to six students each. To help students explore what the Bible says about faith and becoming a Christian, direct their attention to the Treasure Seeker worksheet section titled "Marooned." Ask each team to answer one or more of the questions, making sure all questions are covered. Allow 5 minutes for each question teams must answer. One person in each team should be appointed to record ideas.

Step 2 (7-10 minutes): Have one person from each team explain the team's insights to the rest of

NOTES

the learners. Have students turn to John 1:12. Ask, **What is the result of believing in Jesus, according to John 1:12?** (Becoming children of God or members of God's family.) Explain that "become a son or daughter of God" and "become a member of God's family" are other ways of saying "become a Christian."

Step 3 (7-10 minutes); Ask students to work individually on "Which One Do You Pick?" section of the Treasure Seeker. Allow time for several students to share what they circled as the meaning of "believe," and why.

OPTIONAL (10 minutes)

After completing *Step 3*, lead a discussion with the entire class based on the "Try This" portion of the Treasure Seeker. Have volunteers read the verses aloud and ask for a show of hands for those who wish to express an opinion.

Step 4 (1-2 minutes): Before moving to the Conclusion and Decision part of the session, review the main ideas so far: **What do John 3:16 and John 1:12 say about faith in Jesus?** (It's the way to eternal life and having a family relationship with God.) **What is faith in Jesus?** (Believing He is who He says He is and putting that belief into action by forming a relationship with Him.) Then move to the Conclusion and Decision part of the session.

Conclusion and Decision

CONCLUSION (5-10 minutes)

Tell your students, **Individually read John 3:16 again and paraphrase it in your own words. Then underline the part that means the most to you. It might be the idea that God loves you, or that Jesus died for you. Whatever is especially important to you, mark that part of the verse.**

If time permits, invite volunteers to read their rewrites and share what they underlined as meaning the most to them.

Close in prayer, thanking God for His love and His Son, and asking Him to help you and your students believe in Jesus as Saviour.

Distribute copies of the Fun Page take-home paper. Explain to students that they will receive a new edition after each session. Point out the special

features: the "Earthquake!" maze, the John 3:16 memory verse, and the "Daily Nuggets," which students might wish to follow as a daily devotional guide.

SUGGESTION: Begin a short-term contest (a few weeks) in which students can earn points toward a prize by memorizing John 3:16 and turning in written responses to the "Daily Nuggets." Prizes might be free admission to the next youth group amusement park trip, or a gift certificate at a hobby shop.

SESSION 1

You live on a deserted island. One day you find the words of John 3:16 in a bottle. These are the only words from the Bible you have ever read.

MAROONED

1. What would you know about God?

2. What would you know about His Son?

3. What would you know about the world and the people in it?

4. What would you know about belief?

Which One Do You Pick?

Which of the following groups of words best describes what the Bible means by the word "believe"?

A. **Like, be attached to, be devoted to, feel kindly toward**

B. **Cling to, trust in, rely on, adhere to, stick to**

C. **Cross your fingers and hope to die**

D. **Hope for, wish in, have confidence in, anticipate, desire**

Try This

List the results of believing in Jesus according to these verses:

John 1:12

John 6:40,47

John 11:25,26

John 3:16

Acts 16:30,31

FUN — EARTHQUAKE! — Pages!

A respected scientist has told you that a GIANT EARTHQUAKE is coming. You have only one minute to escape. You are convinced that what the scientist says is true. Does your belief cause a change in your behavior? Yes—it makes you run for the hills!

Run to the hills before you're swallowed up. The roads cross over and under each other.

START

Oops! Uh-oh!

FINISH

Oh, no! Sorry!

If you really believed that the ground was about to split open under your feet, you would run to safety—as fast as your legs could move. In the same way, a strong belief in Jesus Christ will cause a dramatic change in your life. For example, you will want to start doing the things God enjoys—such as helping people in need or telling your friends about fun youth group activities. You will want to drop any wrong things you've been doing. You'll spend time with Him in prayer, think about Him, learn what He is like. To become a Christian is to enter into a whole new way of living. True belief is a dynamic, life-changing thing. How has your life changed since you became a Christian?

DAILY NUGGETS

Wisdom from God's Word for you to read each day.

Day 1   Read John 3:16; 6:40,47; 11:25,27. What is one result of following Jesus?

Day 2   John 1:12. What does it mean to you to be a child of God?

Day 3   John 8:31. What do you learn about the meaning of believing in Jesus?

Day 4   John 16:30,31. What are we to believe about Jesus—in your words?

Day 5   John 7:38. Ask several Christians what this verse means to them. Then write it out in your own words.

Day 6   Romans 6:3,4; 10:9,10. How do you receive new life in Christ?

Hot Tip!

"For God so loved the world that he gave his one and only Son, that whoever believes in him shall not perish but have eternal life."

John 3:16

Stick this verse in your brain for future reference!

POP SHEET

THEME: True belief in Jesus leads to a changed life.

BIBLE STUDY OUTLINE:

Begin your message by relating the story of the rich young ruler found in Matthew 19:16-22. Emphasize the following points, as time allows:

- The meaning of "eternal life" (Verse 16).
- The impossibility of being good enough to keep *all* the commandments in the strength of one's own flesh (see Romans 3:10,23). Ask students if they have never talked back to Mom or Dad!
- The young ruler still felt an emptiness inside, even though he had worked so hard to "please" God. No one can ever be satisfied apart from a personal relationship with God. Only He can fill the emptiness.
- Jesus' demand that the young man sell his possessions was His way of telling him to let go of this world and build his treasure in the next, where it counts.
- Discuss what it means for a modern young person to follow Christ (verse 21).
- The man went away from Christ because his faith did not translate into action—a changed life. This is the main point of this session and the subject of the following object lesson.

NOTES

OBJECT LESSON:
THE FIRECRACKER CHRISTIAN

Preparation: Before class, carefully hollow out a large firecracker so that it cannot ignite or explode. Fill it with gray modeling clay and reinsert the fuse.

After you have told the story of the rich young ruler to your listeners, tell them you want to emphasize the meaning of belief with a visual aid. Show them the firecracker, but don't let them know it is a dud. Describe its deadly potential power. Hold the flame of a lighter near to the fuse, but not near enough to ignite it. Explain to the audience that the firecracker represents the explosive potential of a strong faith in Christ. An "on-fire" Christian can dramatically change the world around him or her—like a stick of dynamite.

Promise the kids you won't really light the fuse. But as you speak, "accidentally" bring the flame into contact with the fuse. As sparks fly out, pretend to panic. Juggle the firecracker in fear, then toss it into the crowd. If your students believe the firecracker is real, they will scream and jump. Restore order to the group by confessing your little deception.

Drive home the idea that true belief in Jesus will cause a dynamic change in a person's life, just as true belief in the explosive danger of a firecracker will make a person run. Point out that it is not enough to have a vague belief in Christ in one's head, but that true belief is demonstrated by the action of new behavior: a changed life.

DISCUSSION QUESTIONS

You may wish to use these questions to stimulate thought and discussion.

1. **What does the rich young man's inability to respond to Christ's demands reveal about his "belief" in God?**
2. **What are some ways a modern young Christian could demonstrate the reality of his or her belief?**
3. **The young man wanted to know how to obtain eternal life. What, according to John 5:24, is the answer? What must a person do?**
4. **Read John 8:31. What is Jesus' instruction to those who say they believe in Him?**

THE COMPLETE JUNIOR HIGH
BIBLE STUDY RESOURCE
BOOK #1

Here are a couple of games to add to your scrap book of physical activities for your young thrill seekers.

"CAR-CAR"

Set up three rows of chairs, as shown.

Leave aisles
between chairs

☐   ☐   ☐

☐   ☐   ☐

☐   ☐   ☐

☐   ☐   ☐

"Rumble Seat"   "Rear Seat"   "Front Seat"

Each row must contain enough chairs to accommodate the number of players. Instruct the players that each row represents a part of a car: the front seat, rear seat, and rumble seat.

To begin the game, seat all players in the "Rear Seat" row. The object of the game is for players to run and be seated in the row which you call out. For example, if you shout, "Rumble seat!" all players must immediately run to that row and sit down. The last player to sit is removed from the game. (To avoid too much rowdiness, anyone who knocks over a chair is also disqualified.) Call another row and again remove the tardy player. As players are eliminated, suddenly inform the remaining people that you are switching the name of each row—the middle row now becomes the "Rumble Seat" and so on. The resulting confusion is fun to watch! Play the game several times and offer small rewards such as candy bars to the victors.

To wear students out, make the spaces between rows very wide.

"CHAIR LIFT"

If your youth room is filled with old, broken down, over-the-hill wooden or metal chairs, have a "chair decorating" contest.

Gather students into small groups. Give each a chair to repair, along with paint and brushes, spray paint, appliques, decals and so forth. Have a box of tools with bolts and screws located centrally.

Challenge teams to create the very "best" chair. You, the judge, will award some reward or honor to the winners. You may wish to make these "theme" chairs, reflecting the subject of your Bible message.

WARNING: Be sure to cover the floor, to control all paint and brushes, and to have the permission of the people in charge of the church furniture!

SOME OTHER THINGS YOU CAN TRY:

1. Create a "Chair-riot" relay race by having teams carry a person in a chariot made of one chair with two broomsticks for handles.

2. Play "Musical Chairs." (It's still fun.) For a variation, cover the floor with a plastic tarp that has been smeared with grease. Have kids run in bare feet.

3. Have a "chair stuffing" contest: challenge teams to see which can seat the most people on one chair. Sitting on laps is fair. WARNING: Use sturdy chairs.

Benefits

WHAT THE SESSION IS ABOUT

The benefits of being a Christian include salvation, forgiveness, access to God's power, protection, and membership in God's family.

SCRIPTURE STUDIED

Psalm 103:12; Luke 24:49; John 6:47; Acts 1:8; Romans 1:16; 10:9; 1 Corinthians 10:13; Ephesians 2:19; 6:11; 1 Thessalonians 5:9; 2 Timothy 1:7; Hebrews 8:12.

KEY PASSAGE

"I pray also that the eyes of your heart may be enlightened in order that you may know the hope to which he has called you, the riches of his glorious inheritance in the saints, and his incomparably great power for us who believe."

Ephesians 1:18,19

AIMS OF THE SESSION

1. List five benefits of believing in Jesus.
2. Consider ways that these benefits apply to people today.
3. Express thanks to God for these benefits.

INSIGHTS FOR THE LEADER

This session focuses on the benefits that God gives His children. As your students explore the Scripture they will discover that some of these benefits are salvation, forgiveness, protection, power, and belonging to the family of God. The purpose of this session is to give learners a quick introduction to these concepts. Later sessions will allow time for more detailed exploration.

Salvation is the point at which a person enters into God's benefits; without salvation, one is not eligible for the other benefits. Salvation means deliverance and safety. When God saves us, He delivers us from the penalty of sin and offers us His protection from its power in our lives. "For God did not appoint us to suffer wrath but to receive salvation through our Lord Jesus Christ" (1 Thess. 5:9).

God cannot simply excuse sin, or ignore it. If we were left on our own, we would not be able to please God or come up to His standards, and so we would have to suffer the penalty of our sin (see Rom. 3:23). But God loves us so much that He Himself provided the solution. Christ's death on the cross satisfied the need for payment of the penalty (see Rom. 5:8).

The way to receive salvation is to believe in Christ. As He Himself said: "I tell you the truth, he who believes has everlasting life" (John 6:47). The apostle Paul also stressed the importance of belief: "I am not ashamed of the gospel, because it is the power of God for the salvation of everyone who believes: first for the Jew, then for the Gentile" (Rom. 1:16); "That if you confess with your mouth, 'Jesus is Lord,' and believe in your heart that God raised him from the dead, you will be saved" (Rom. 10:9).

Junior highers may need help in understanding the benefits of salvation, since they tend to think in terms of the concrete and the temporal. They will probably state the main benefit as "going to heaven." This benefits us when we die, but there are benefits for here and now, too. Learners will probably also be able to state that with salvation Jesus comes into our hearts and lives. His presence is a benefit that believers grow to appreciate more and more as time passes.

There are many other benefits of salvation—too many to deal with in one session or even a full course. But this session touches on several more: forgiveness, power, protection, and belonging to God's family.

Forgiveness is an important benefit. When we are reborn to new life, we receive God's unconditional and complete forgiveness. However, we may still commit sin. And while this will not affect our position as children of God, it will certainly affect our fellowship with Him. Therefore, when we sin we need His forgiveness. During the Bible Exploration, students will study God's promise that when we

confess our sins, He will forgive us and cleanse us from our unrighteousness (see 1 John 1:9).

A helpful analogy might be taking a shower after getting really dirty and sweaty. It feels good to get clean! Similarly, being cleansed from our sins makes us feel clean and fresh inside. Another way of looking at it is having a weight lifted from our shoulders. The weight of sin some people carry around can be very heavy and burdensome. Confessing and receiving forgiveness can be a great relief.

Forgiveness means more than just feeling better. God Himself, when He forgives us, "will remember [our] sins no more" (Heb. 8:12). He doesn't just forgive, He forgets. This point comes across forcefully in Psalm 103:12: "As far as the east is from the west, so far has he removed our transgressions from us."

A person could travel around the world going east and would never suddenly be going west. (If someone traveled far enough north, he or she would come to the north pole and would have to start traveling south.) When God forgives our sins, He removes them so far from us that we can never meet up with them again.

Making comparisons with human relationships will help young people see the importance of being forgiven. They have probably experienced the uncomfortable situation of having someone who is angry with them but who refuses to forgive them. It is unpleasant and depressing. If God refused to forgive, we would be condemned to eternal punishment; but God does forgive! And so junior highers can confess and receive His forgiveness. Their sins need no longer weigh them down, and they can be liberated to serve God and concentrate on getting to know Him better.

Access to God's power is another benefit of salvation learners will discover in their exploration of Scripture. Access comes by approaching Jesus Christ and asking to be filled with the Holy Spirit from whom comes such power. Jesus promised, "You will receive power when the Holy Spirit comes on you; and you will be my witnesses" (Acts 1:8). Earlier He had told the disciples, "I am going to send you what my Father has promised; but stay in the city until you have been clothed with power from on high" (Luke 24:49). He knew that His followers would not be able, in their own strength, to carry His message throughout the world. So He sends the Holy Spirit to live in Christians and give them the power they need. The Spirit helps believers to overcome their fear about witnessing, because "God did not give us a spirit of timidity, but a spirit of power, of love and of self-discipline" (2 Tim. 1:7). It is *His* strength, not their own, that enables Christians to be His witnesses.

Protection is a vital part of God's "benefit package" for His people. Learners will find in their study that God protects them when they are tempted. "No temptation has seized you except what is common to man. And God is faithful; he will not let you be tempted beyond what you can bear. But when you are tempted, he will also provide a way out so that you can stand up under it" (1 Cor. 10:13). Our Lord does not leave us to struggle alone against the pull of temptation: He provides the help we need. He also provides protection against Satan's attacks: "Put on the full armor of God so that you can take your stand against the devil's schemes" (Eph. 6:11). As explained in the remaining verses of Ephesians 6, God's armor includes truth, righteousness, the gospel, faith, salvation, and the Word of God. If junior highers take advantage of their armor, they will be protected against the tricks Satan will try to pull on them.

Finally, God gives His children **membership in His family**. Christians do not have to "make it" on their own. "You are no longer foreigners and aliens, but fellow citizens with God's people and members of God's household" (Eph. 2:19). Christian teens can have fun together without the negative influences of drugs, profanity, and pressure for sexual involvement. They can enjoy talking about Christ together. They can help and teach each other. Young people may also enjoy fellowship with believers of other ages, both younger and older. Parents, teachers, and church staff can help learners grow in Christ and overcome problems. God's family offers young people a sense of belonging and of being someone who is important to God and to their brothers and sisters in Christ.

SESSION PLAN

BEFORE CLASS BEGINS: Follow the instructions on the "Benefit Puzzle" Teaching Resource Page (next to this session's student worksheet.)

Attention Grabber

ATTENTION GRABBER (5-10 minutes)

Give each arriving student one picture from the Teaching Resource. When you are ready to begin class, tell students, **I have handed out copies of three different pictures: a knee, a kid throwing a fit, and a bee.** (If your classroom is soundproof and you wish to get your students "charged up," lead a shouting contest between the three groups of students to see which can shout the name of their picture the loudest.) Then say, **If we put these three pictures in the proper order, they will spell an important word. Let's see who can be the first to figure it out.** Write the words on your chalkboard or overhead projector in this order: knee, fit, bee. Challenge students to shout out the proper order that will produce the answer, *benefit*.

Ask students, **Suppose you inherited a million dollars. What benefits would it provide for you now and in the future?** Let students discuss. If they need help, suggest ideas such as these: You would be self-sufficient, so you wouldn't have to work. You could buy anything you needed or wanted. You wouldn't need to attend school in order to learn enough to make a living (though you might want to continue your education

for the satisfaction of learning). Let students have fun with this one. Then sum up with a comment on the meaning of the word "benefit." Make a transition to the next part of the lesson by saying, **We've been talking about the benefits of having a million dollars. But there's something in life that gives even greater benefits, and we're going to see what that is.**

25

Bible Exploration

EXPLORATION (15-25 minutes)

Step 1 (7-10 minutes): Direct students' attention to "God Gives Us" on the student worksheet. Have them work individually to complete the suggested activities, look up the Scriptures, and determine the benefits God gives His people. Be available to answer questions and encourage learners.

Step 2 (8-15 minutes): Using the suggestions that follow, guide a discussion of the benefits students discovered in Scripture and help them understand implications for life today.

Ask, **Who will tell us their answer for the first one?** (You are looking for "salvation"; if students suggest equivalent phrases such as "becoming a Christian" ask, "What's another word for that?")

Ask, **What does salvation mean? How do we get it? Why is it a benefit? What does God do for us when He saves us?**

Move on to the next benefit, *forgiveness*. (The worksheet lists the following benefits in random order.) Ask for students' responses to the activity. Then ask, **Why is it important to us to be forgiven by God? What would happen if He did not forgive us? How do you feel when a parent or friend refuses to forgive you? How do you feel when they forgive you?** Remind students that God's forgiveness goes beyond feelings, important as those are. Being forgiven by God actually frees us from the guilt and penalty of sin and allows us to concentrate on living for Him instead of worrying about our sins.

Move on to the next benefit, *power*. **What kind of power does God give?** (Power to witness for Him.) **What are some ways God's power has enabled you to be His witness? What are some ways you would like to have more of His power for witnessing?**

Move on to the next benefit, *protection.* **What do the verses tell you about God's protection?** (God promises to protect us from any temptation that is too great for us to resist.)

The final benefit is *belonging to the family of God*—our brothers and sisters in Christ. **What are the benefits of being in a family with Christian brothers and sisters? What are some ways other Christians have helped you with something that was difficult or impossible to do on your own? What does it mean to you to be able to meet and talk with people who love the Lord as you do?**

Summarize the discussion by saying something like this: **God gives us salvation, forgiveness of sins, His power and protection, a family of believers. I hope these benefits excite you as much as they do me!** Then move to the CONCLUSION, or to the OPTIONAL STEP.

OPTIONAL STEP (5-10 minutes)

Direct students to "A Reason to Believe." Have them work individually to think about the benefits of being a Christian that they have examined, and then decide how to answer the letter in the student guide. When they have completed their answers, have several read them. Summarize by saying, **We have seen some of the benefits that God gives His people. We have seen that He gives us salvation, forgiveness, protection, power, and membership in His family. In later sessions we will examine these benefits in more detail. Right now, an appropriate response would be to thank Him for what He has done for us.** Then move to the CONCLUSION.

Conclusion and Decision

CONCLUSION (5 minutes)

Have students work individually. Instruct them to choose one benefit that means the most to them and then to write a short "telegram" to God explaining why they appreciate that particular benefit and to thank Him for each one.

Close in prayer and distribute the Fun Page take-home paper as students leave.

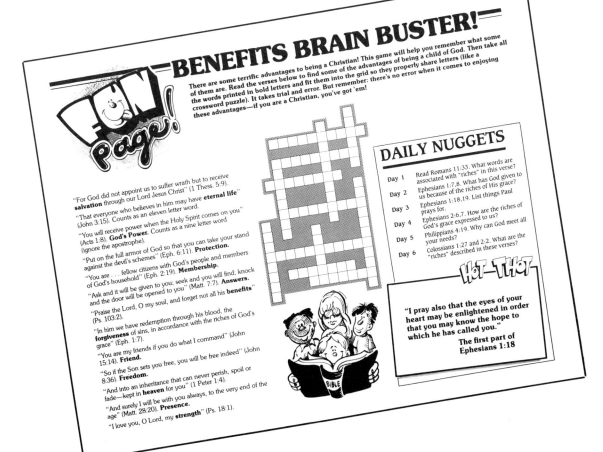

Your students may wish to see this solution to the Fun Page puzzle.

(If you like, write the solution on an extra copy of the Fun Page and pin it to your classroom bulletin board.)

NOTE: The next session requires several rubber stamp ink pads and stamped envelopes.

27

Treasure Seeker

God Gives Us

Read the verses listed below. Fill in the blanks with the appropriate words that describe the benefits of being a Christian. Study the cartoons (and fiil them out) to get the benefit being described in the verses.

John 6:47
God gives us _____

ADMIT ONE The HEAVEN–BOUND EXPRESS

Departure times are unannounced
Serving: Heaven, Paradise and Kingdom Com—

TICKETHOLDER

1 Corinthians 10:13
God gives us _____

Draw yourself in the driver's seat.

SPLAT!

SPLIT!

Ephesians 2:19
God gives us _____

Write in the cartoon balloons the name of a Christian person you know who fits the age category illustrated.

Colossians 1:10,11
God gives us _____

Complete the mini dot-to-dot

1 John 1:9
God gives us _____
List all your sins that GOD REMEMBERS here: ☐

A Reason to Believe

You received a letter from a friend saying, "What's so good about being a Christian? It just seems like there would be nothing in it for me. I'd be glad to talk to you about it some more if I had a reason to believe."

Please respond by writing a letter on the back of this sheet telling your friend about the benefits of being a Christian.

Benefit Puzzle

Cut out these pictures. Shuffle them and hand them out one card per person as students arrive at class. If necessary, photocopy this page so that there are enough pictures for your class. See the session's Attention Grabber activity for further instructions.

BENEFITS BRAIN BUSTER!

There are some terrific advantages to being a Christian! This game will help you remember what some of them are. Read the verses below to find some of the advantages of being a child of God. Then take all the words printed in bold letters and fit them into the grid so they properly share letters (like a crossword puzzle). It takes trial and error. But remember: there's no error when it comes to enjoying these advantages—if you are a Christian, you've got 'em!

"For God did not appoint us to suffer wrath but to receive **salvation** through our Lord Jesus Christ" (1 Thess. 5:9).

"That everyone who believes in him may have **eternal life**" (John 3:15). Counts as an eleven letter word.

"You will receive power when the Holy Spirit comes on you" (Acts 1:8). **God's Power.** Counts as a nine letter word (ignore the apostrophe).

"Put on the full armor of God so that you can take your stand against the devil's schemes" (Eph. 6:11). **Protection.**

"You are . . . fellow citizens with God's people and members of God's household" (Eph. 2:19). **Membership.**

"Ask and it will be given to you; seek and you will find; knock and the door will be opened to you" (Matt. 7:7). **Answers.**

"Praise the Lord, O my soul, and forget not all his **benefits**" (Ps. 103:2).

"In him we have redemption through his blood, the **forgiveness** of sins, in accordance with the riches of God's grace" (Eph. 1:7).

"You are my friends if you do what I command" (John 15:14). **Friend.**

"So if the Son sets you free, you will be free indeed" (John 8:36). **Freedom.**

"And into an inheritance that can never perish, spoil or fade—kept in **heaven** for you" (1 Peter 1:4).

"And surely I will be with you always, to the very end of the age" (Matt. 28:20). **Presence.**

"I love you, O Lord, my **strength**" (Ps. 18:1).

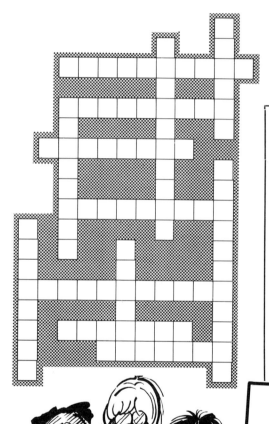

DAILY NUGGETS

Day 1　Read Romans 11:33. What words are associated with "riches" in this verse?

Day 2　Ephesians 1:7,8. What has God given to us because of the riches of His grace?

Day 3　Ephesians 1:18,19. List things Paul prays for.

Day 4　Ephesians 2:6,7. How are the riches of God's grace expressed to us?

Day 5　Philippians 4:19. Why can God meet all your needs?

Day 6　Colossians 1:27 and 2:2. What are the "riches" described in these verses?

HOT THOT

"I pray also that the eyes of your heart may be enlightened in order that you may know the hope to which he has called you."

The first part of Ephesians 1:18

 POP SHEET

THE COMPLETE JUNIOR HIGH BIBLE STUDY RESOURCE BOOK #1
© 1987 GL/LIGHT FORCE, VENTURA, CA 93006

THEME: The benefits of being a Christian far outweigh the benefits of being the richest fool on earth. A Christian who is centered on God has no need to worry.

BIBLE STUDY OUTLINE

Tell the parable of the rich fool (Luke 12:15-34). Emphasize the following points as time allows:

- The significance of Christ's command to "watch out" (*see verse* 15). He means for us to be ready, alert, prepared; implies an active danger is present. Christians can be tempted away from their Lord by the things of this world.
- "Take life easy; eat, drink and be merry" (*see verse* 19). This is the world's philosophy. Contrast it to the fact that each Christian has a God-given purpose in this world and that each life therefore has the potential for eternally important impact. Also, the non-Christian can strive to be merry, but only a child of God can experience the joy of knowing Him.
- "You fool!" (*see verse* 20). This man was declared to be a fool— and when God calls you a fool, you're a fool! God labeled the rich man useless because he was not "rich toward God" (as it says in verse 21).
- Verses 22-31 speak of *focus*. When a person's life is focused on the world, all he or she can do is worry about the so-called necessities of life. But a person who is focused on God will soon find that He supplies these things and much more (*see verse* 31).
- Verse 32 tells us that God is actually *pleased* to give us the eternal kingdom and all its benefits and wonders. Nothing can prevent Him from blessing us, unless *we* refuse to seek Him (*see* verse 31).
- The key to all this is the Christian's *heart* (refer to verse 34). If a person's heart treasures the world, then that person is a fool just like the rich fool. But a person who loves God will prosper.

OBJECT LESSON: TELESCOPE

Show a telescope or magnifying lens to your listeners as you speak about being focused on God. You may wish to allow students to look through the telescope.

DISCUSSION QUESTIONS

1. **What did the rich man plan to do?**
2. **Did he include God in his plans?**
3. **What is the difference between being merry and having joy?**
4. **According to verse 21, what was the rich man's mistake?**
5. **How can a person be rich toward God?**
6. **Name several practical things a Christian should be doing to remain focused on God.**
7. **Do you have plans for your future and, if so, are you including God in your plans?**
8. **What would you need to do to start including Him in your plans?**
9. **Name some of the benefits of being a Christian, both now and in heaven.**

 NOTES

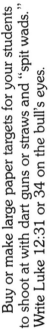

THE COMPLETE JUNIOR HIGH
BIBLE STUDY RESOURCE
BOOK #1

To help drive home to your students the idea that a Christian needs to focus or target his or her life on God, play some of these games.

You can build a simple ring toss game by pounding nails part way into a sheet of plywood. Label the nails with different values of points. Players attempt to hook nails by throwing a small loop of rope.

If your group has access to BB guns or pellet rifles, hang Christmas tree balls to the nails of your ring toss game and let players shoot them to pieces.

And don't forget the old "win a goldfish" carnival game. Players try to toss a coin or other object into a cup surrounded by cups. You could put a candy bar or other prize in the cup.

Buy or make large paper targets for your students to shoot at with dart guns or straws and "spit wads." Write Luke 12:31 or 34 on the bull's eyes.

"EGG FACE"

There are a lot of great games that can be played with eggs. Here's a real crowd-pleaser that goes along with the idea of being on target.

Ask for six volunteers—three girls and three boys. The boys lay on their backs on the floor, each with a paper cup in his mouth. The girls each stand on a chair and hold their egg at arms length as shown in the illustration.

The object is to break the shell and drop the contents into the cup without splashing the boy. This is a very messy game, so have the boys remove their shirts and lie on a plastic drop cloth. Provide towels and water for clean up, and be sure to have a trash can so the girls can immediately toss the eggshells away.

Suggestion: eggs are sometimes hard to break with fingers, so allow girls to crack them against the chairs.

Games that require a player to find a target while blindfolded (such as "Pin the Tail on the Donkey") can make the point that Christians must not blindly grope through life but instead keep their eyes wide open and on God. You might try challenging players to pin a paper heart on a poster of Luke 12:34. Or play an old-fashioned piñata game. You can also use blindfolds with any of the games suggested above.

Commitment

WHAT THE SESSION IS ABOUT

Christ demands a life-changing commitment from those who believe in Him.

SCRIPTURE STUDIED

Matthew 10:37,38; Mark 12:30; Luke 6:46-49; John 8:31; 14:15.

KEY PASSAGE

"Why do you call me, 'Lord, Lord,' and do not do what I say?"
Luke 6:46

AIMS OF THE SESSION

During this session your learners will:
1. Understand that a Christian must be committed to Christ.
2. Examine Jesus' teaching on the committed Christian life.
3. Commit to one specific area of obedience to God.

INSIGHTS FOR THE LEADER

In Session 2 you and your students studied some of the benefits of being a Christian. Now it's time to look at the *responsibilities* involved in the Christian life. This session will challenge your young people to consider committing themselves wholly to God.

Obedience

Obeying Jesus' commands is the first way of giving one's life to Him. He said that if we really love Him, we will obey His commands (see John 14:15). He also made it clear that lip service is not adequate: "Why do you call me, 'Lord, Lord,' and do not do what I say?" (Luke: 6:46). It is not enough to call Him Lord without making any effort to obey Him. In fact, one who does so is like a person who builds a house without a foundation. When a flood comes, the house will collapse (see Luke 6:49). In contrast, the person who comes to Jesus, hears His words, and puts them into practice is building a solid life. "He is like a man building a house, who dug down deep and laid the foundation on rock. When a flood came, the torrent struck that house but could not shake it, because it was well built" (Luke 6:48). This person is reaching his full potential as a human being and as a Christian, because he is living God's way and allowing the Lord to show him what is best for him. When life's problems hit him, he will not collapse, because his commitment to the Lord has placed him on a solid foundation.

Jesus also tied our love for Him to our obedience. He said, "If you love me, you will obey what I command" (John 14:15). Our love for Him will make us want to do what pleases Him; and His love for us will cause Him to ask us to do only what is best for us.

He Knows What's Best

Jesus also said, "If you hold to my teaching, you are really my disciples" (John 8:31). **Holding to His teaching means believing the truths of the gospel as well as obeying the Lord's instructions.** It's important to believe the truths, because they give us confidence that God loves us and that He knows what He is doing when He commands us to do certain things. Obeying His instructions is important because He knows what is best. Often small children will rebel against a parent's instructions and commands. They wonder why they can't run into the street or play with matches. But parents know that these actions are dangerous, and so they make sure the children don't do them. Good parents try to make sure children eat the right foods, get enough sleep, and so on. Our heavenly Father gives us instructions that are meant for our own good and that will give us the best possible life.

NOTES

Love

Another important point to get across to junior highers is that **a Christian's love for God, which leads him or her to obey God, is more than just an emotion.** We have difficulty controlling our emotions, and sometimes they are not what we would like them to be. Jesus said, "Love the Lord your God with all your heart and with all your soul and with all your mind and with all your strength" (Mark 12:30). Even when a person is having a hard time *feeling* love for God, he or she can love God with other parts of the being that are not emotions. He can love God with his strength by helping weaker people. She can love God with her mind by doing her best in school and by studying the Bible regularly. Love may be expressed in many ways and at many levels besides the emotional level.

Another aspect of commitment that your learners will discover in their Scripture search is **Jesus' demand that we place Him above our human relationships.** He said, "Anyone who loves his father or mother more than me is not worthy of me; anyone who loves his son or daughter more than me is not worthy of me" (Matt. 10:37). That includes best friends and friends of the opposite sex. Junior highers may let a group of non-Christian friends persuade them to go roller skating instead of going to a church activity; or they may feel embarrassed when unchurched friends ask them what they're doing on a certain evening when the answer is "Going to youth group at church." One of the costs of discipleship is to value our relationship with God so highly that all human relationships take second place.

Commitment to Jesus Christ takes time. It is a process, not something that happens instantly. The process takes place day by day as believers allow the Holy Spirit to transform them by renewing their minds, as Paul said in Romans 12:1,2. In order for this to happen, your learners need to read the Bible and pray regularly. This will put them in touch with God and with His transforming ministry. When they do this, everything they experience can be used by the Lord to make them more and more Christlike and thus more fully committed to Him.

SESSION PLAN

BEFORE CLASS BEGINS: The EXPLORATION calls for rubber stamp ink pads, one for every three or four students. The CONCLUSION requires a stamped envelope for each student.

Attention Grabber

ATTENTION GRABBER (5-7 minutes)

As students arrive have them write on the chalkboard or on butcher paper the sound made by a pet they own or have owned.

When you are ready to begin class, ask students to name some of the benefits of owning a family pet such as a dog. (Answers could include companionship, protection, a playmate.) Then ask the students to identify some of the responsibilities of owning a pet. (Feeding, cleaning up after, trips to the vet, training, and so on.)

Now say something like this: **As you can see, there are benefits and responsibilities** involved in owning a pet. During our last Bible study we examined some of the benefits of being a Christian—salvation, forgiveness, God's power and protection, and membership in God's family. Now it's time for us to talk about some of our responsibilities as Christians. Today we will look at *commitment:* the fact that we must give our lives completely to God.

CREATIVE OPTION (10-12 minutes)

When students have arrived, walk them outside to your car. Ask students to name some of the benefits of owning a car and a driver's license (ability to go where you wish, take friends along, no more bus rides). Now point to various parts of your car and ask students to describe the responsibilities involved: The steering wheel (drive safely); the gas tank filler cap (cost of operation); the gas pedal (observing traffic laws); the engine (maintenance); the tires (air); the seat belts (safety); the chrome (cleaning). You could also mention cost of insurance.

As everyone walks back to the classroom, describe how that just as there are benefits to being a Christian, there are responsibilities, too. Say, **Today we are going to talk about a very important responsibility: anyone who wants to be a Christian must commit his or her life fully to the Lord.**

Bible Exploration

EXPLORATION (20-25 minutes)

Materials needed: Rubber stamp ink pads (in various colors if you like), one for each group of three or four students; one Treasure Seeker per group; paper towels or pre-moistened towelettes to clean learners' fingers.

Move students into groups and distribute worksheets. Tell students to answer the seven questions on the Treasure Seeker. As students work, move about the room to help students and to distribute ink pads when groups have answered all questions. Encourage young people to have fun making their cartoons.

When everyone is finished, collect worksheets and display the comic strips for all to see. Lead a class discussion based on the seven questions on the Treasure Seeker to be sure everyone has a clear understanding of the need for Christians to commit themselves to obey the Lord. After students suggest some responses to question seven, areas where young people have trouble being obedient to the Lord, ask for some ideas for dealing with these problem areas.

SUGGESTION: If you have access to a photocopier which enlarges, make posters of the students' comic strip. You can make them very big by multiple enlargements on several sheets of paper which are then taped together to form a complete picture. Display posters for all to see during the next class time.

Conclusion and Decision

CONCLUSION (5-10 minutes)

Materials needed: A stamped envelope and a sheet of writing paper for each student.

Say, **Write a letter to yourself about one area of obedience to God which you need to improve. This might be a simple thing like taking out the trash without griping or a more difficult thing such as giving up a bad habit or a crowd of people that doesn't help your spiritual life. This is to be a personal time of thought about your commitment to discipleship. No one will read your letter but yourself.**

After students finish their letters, give them stamped envelopes. Have them seal the letter in the envelope and write their names and addresses on the outside. Collect the letters and hold them, unopened, for a month. Then mail them to the students.

Close in prayer. As students leave, distribute the Fun Page take-home paper.

NOTE: The next session requires a potted plant and other materials. See the note on page 48 for details.

Treasure Seeker

Thumb Things Happening Here

These questions will help you discover some of the responsibilities of being a Christian.

1. John 14:15 says, "If you love me, you will _____."

2. According to John 8:31, what must you do to really be a disciple (follower) of Christ?

3. What four things are you to commit to the God you love? (Mark 12:30)

4. According to Matthew 10:37 we should love God (check one):

   ☐ less than we love our family

   ☐ more than we love our family

   ☐ as much as we love our family

5. Matthew 10:38 tells us we must take up our cross and follow Jesus. Taking up our cross means (circle one):

   A. carry around a large wooden cross.

   B. live with all the problems you have.

   C. be willing to follow Jesus even unto death.

6. If we really want Jesus to be our Lord what must we commit ourselves to do, according to Luke 6:46?

7. As you can see, Jesus made it clear that we are to obey Him. List three things that a Christian your age might have trouble doing (for example, a regular time of Bible study).

Now for some fun—or should we say *thumb* fun? Create your own "thumbprint art" comic strip based on the story Jesus told of houses built on rock and sand (Luke 6:47-49). Work with your friends to write the dialogue, then create the cartoon characters by drawing arms and legs and faces on your thumbprints. In the last panel, write a definition of *commitment* based on your comic strip. Use a sheet of blank paper for your cartoon.

FUN page!

THE COMMITMENT CLUE!

A▸

Fold so that arrows **A** and **B** meet points **A** and **B**, as shown.

●A

What does the word "commitment" mean?

If you happen to be carrying a dictionary in your backpack, you can look it up. Or you can fold this page as shown in the illustration so that the answer will appear before your very eyes.

B▸

●B

Speech bubbles from comic:

"COMET MINT"? A NEW CANDY, RIGHT?

"COMET MINT"? "KERMIT MUTT"? TOAD LIPS! GET SERIOUS!

IS A TELEVISION DOG PUPPET SHOW!

I MUST SAY, I ENTIRELY DISAGREE. MOREOVER, FRIENDS, I TRUST YOU SEE THAT A "CO-MITT-MITT" IS MADE FOR A THREE-HANDED BASEBALL PLAYER

MY DAD KNOWS WHAT IT MEANS HE WAS A SAFE-CRACKER—NOW HE'S COMMITTED TO JAIL!

KEEP QUIET! DON'T TALK! I WANT TO GO ON SLEEPING!

If you have committed your life to God, it's probably because you have confidence in Him— confidence that He will guide you and guard you as a loving parent does a child. Trust God. He won't let you down.

DAILY NUGGETS

Wisdom from God's Word for you to read each day.

Day 1 Read 1 John 2:3-6. How do we show that we know Jesus? If you are going to live as Jesus did, how will you find out how He lived?

Day 2 1 John 2:9-11. How can people tell whether or not you are living in the light? Name one specific action you could take to show love to someone.

Day 3 1 John 2:15-17. What are some of the things in the world that take you away from God?

Day 4 1 John 3:16-20. According to verse 18, how are we to show our love for one another?

Day 5 1 John 5:3. How do we show our love for God?

Day 6 Ephesians 5:8-10. What is one way you can find out what pleases the Lord?

If you put this in one ear, make sure it doesn't come out the other.

"Why do you call me, 'Lord, Lord,' and do not do what I say?"

Luke 6:46

THEME: Christ demands a life-changing commitment from those who believe in Him.

BIBLE STUDY OUTLINE:

The passage you will examine is Luke 14:28-30; the parable of the unwise builder. Begin your message by relating the story of some project you once attempted but left unfinished because it was too hard or costly. Then read the passage, making the following observations as time allows:

- The background of the passage (Jesus talking to the crowds).
- The sort of people who made up the crowds (disciples, self-righteous, hangers-on, unbelievers, needy).
- Jesus was talking about the cost of discipleship. Point out that to be a disciple of Christ (His student, His follower) requires *commitment*. Talk about the nature of commitment (requires strength and backbone, usually means to go against the crowd, etc.).
- Discuss the necessity of counting the cost of discipleship, of deciding whether the Christian life is worth the price of losing non-Christian friends and other such problems.

DISCUSSION QUESTIONS

If your audience is responsive, use these to stimulate thinking.

1. **If you were a member of the crowd Jesus spoke to, would you be a disciple, a hanger-on, an unbeliever, a spiritually needy person, or what?** (This is a rhetorical question.)
2. **What was it about the disciples in the crowd that made them different from the others?**
3. **What is it about us today that sets us apart from the crowd?**
4. **If to be a disciple of Christ means to follow Him and study Him, what are some things a person must do or not do to be His disciple?**
5. **Is it sometimes hard to be a disciple? Why or why not?**
6. **What are some things we could do as a group to make it easier for each of us to remain committed to discipleship and to Christ?**

SPECIAL PROJECT

Draw the following chart on a large piece of poster paper or on the chalkboard or overhead projector. Hand out pencils and paper for students to make their own copies to keep. (Or make an 8½″ × 11″ version and run off copies for your students.)

THE DISCIPLESHIP COMMITMENT CONTRACT				
Commitment	Passage	Daily or Weekly	Time	Comments
PRAYER	1 Thess. 5:17			
BIBLE STUDY	2 Tim. 3:16			
BIBLE MEMORIZATION	Psalm 119:11			
FELLOWSHIP	Acts 2:42			
THANKSGIVING	1 Thess. 5:18			
CONFESSION	1 John 1:9			
WORSHIP	Psalm 100:2			
GIVING	2 Cor. 9:6,7			
SPECIAL PROJECT:				

This chart is a "contract" between each student and God. The "Commitment" column lists things a person should do to be a strong, growing Christian. Your students are to individually fill out this chart as an indication of their commitment to God. Help them by reading the appropriate Bible passages as you go over the several categories. "Daily or Weekly" refers to how frequently each student will perform the item under "Commitment." Under "Time" the students should write the amount of time they intend to spend performing each item. Save the "Special Project" until all students have finished filling out the contract.

Lead a discussion concerning special things your class could do as an outpouring of Christian love and concern. (Visit shut-ins, mount a food drive, organize a retreat for handicapped children, etc.) Choose one your class will do and have everyone work together to plan the details.

Have the students sign their contracts.

THE COMPLETE JUNIOR HIGH
BIBLE STUDY RESOURCE
BOOK #1

Stick these games in your Bag of Tricks.

"KNEE TACKLE"

THIS GAME IS FOR JUNIOR HIGH BOYS ONLY!

(Older kids will hurt themselves.) Participants must wear kneepads and old clothes. Playing field must be grass, with no dangerous sprinkler heads.

Mark off a playing field about 25 by 50 feet and line up teams as shown in the illustration.

The game is called "Knee Tackle" because all players must always remain on their knees. The object is for teams to score points by advancing the ball (football or softball) across the opponents' goal line. The defending team attempts to stop the progress of the offense by tackling the ball carrier. A player is not considered tackled until he declares himself "dead," i.e., it is impossible for him to move under the weight of the opponents or for him to hand the ball off.

The offense has four plays in which to cross the goal line. They may pass or "run." They may even roll the ball from player to player since the ball is never dead until the carrier yells "dead." If the offense fails to cross the goal line in four plays, the defense takes over the ball. The ball must be **carried** over the goal line or thrown to a receiver in the end zone to score points. Seven points are awarded for each touchdown. This is a rough game, so keep a close eye on the tempers and keep each game short. You might wish to make up your own rules and penalties as you go along.

VARIATIONS:

Try your own versions of "Knee Basketball" (rope a bucket to a tree for the basketball hoop), and "Knee Baseball" with a Whiffle ball and bat. Many of the standard games your youth group plays can be done on knees—especially relay races. But always remember to use kneepads!

"RELAY RATS"

Speaking of relay races, it seems that the "rats" in most youth groups can never get enough of relay races and their almost endless variations. Here are a couple of good old standbys you may not have done in awhile:

1. Two players pull another on a blanket as shown.

2. Players must run while covered with a sleeping bag.

3. Two of these simple props make for a fun race:

Ingredients for Growth SESSION 4

WHAT THE SESSION IS ABOUT

Five ingredients for growth: Bible study, Bible memorization, prayer, confession, and fellowship.

SCRIPTURE STUDIED

Psalm 119:11; Luke 18:1; Acts 2:42; 2 Timothy 2:15, 3:16; 1 John 1:7,9.

KEY PASSAGE

"So then, just as you received Christ Jesus as Lord, continue to live in him." Colossians 2:6

AIMS OF THE SESSION

During this session your learners will:

1. List five practices that help a Christian grow and at least three things that stop growth.
2. Discuss ways in which the five practices contribute to a Christian's growth.
3. Plan a way to improve in an area where growth is needed.

INSIGHTS FOR THE LEADER

In this session your students will be introduced to the following practices which are necessary for personal spiritual growth. Many of these actions will be covered in greater depth during later sessions.

1. Bible Study. Reading God's Word and thinking about it will allow your students to receive God's message for them. His message "is useful for teaching, rebuking, correcting and training in righteousness" (2 Tim. 3:16). He encourages His children to correctly handle the word of truth (see 2 Tim. 2:15).

Your students may have some difficulty in developing a regular habit of Bible study. An easy-to-understand version and a not-too-ambitious reading schedule may help junior highers discover the strength of a consistent time in the Word.

2. Bible Memory. Hiding God's Word in their hearts will give young people added resources to resist temptation and to know what is right and wrong in their daily living. "Thy word I have treasured in my heart, that I may not sin against Thee" (Ps. 119:11, NASB). As they face temptation, they will recall Scriptures that show them how to resist. Memorized Scripture also gives them something to share with friends when witnessing or when fellowshipping with other believers, and will provide guidance for many decisions.

Junior highers can usually memorize well. The most difficult task is developing the incentive to memorize. Some groups use contests or games to encourage memory of the Word.

3. Prayer. "Jesus told his disciples a parable to show them that they should always pray and not give up" (Luke 18:1). Talking to God is an important part of communication with the Father. Point out that your students can talk to God any time. They don't have to pray only on special occasions, or in a certain posture.

It is important for young people to understand that prayer is not presenting a shopping list of requests. It is conversing with a loving God. People who love each other don't communicate only in requests; they may share what has been happening in their lives, or express their affection for one another. When one person does make a request, the other may or may not find it appropriate to grant that request. Similarly, when Christians make requests in prayer, our Father will grant the request if it is in our best interests and fits in with His plans. But He may say no if He knows that the denial will be better for us. Or He may say, "Wait awhile."

Junior highers will grow as they learn to communicate with God and gain experience in the ways in which He answers various prayers. Although junior highers are often timid about praying out loud, you can encourage them to pray silently at any time.

4. Confession of sins. Young people need to get their lives cleaned up in order to

walk in fellowship with God. Confession opens the door to God's forgiveness and cleansing. Scripture says, "If we confess our sins, he is faithful and just and will forgive us our sins and purify us from all unrighteousness" (1 John 1:9). He forgets the sins that are confessed (see Heb. 8:12) and removes them from us as far as the east is from the west (see Ps. 103:12).

Encourage students to confess each sin as they become aware of it. Junior highers may store up a number of sins to confess "later," but this is not helpful to Christian growth. Unconfessed sin hinders the Christian's fellowship with the Lord (see Isa. 59:1,2).

5. Fellowship. Scripture tells us that the early Christians "were continually devoting themselves to the apostles' teaching and to fellowship, to the breaking of bread and to prayer" (Acts 2:42, *NASB*). Fellowship is an important part of the Christian experience. It involves a sharing of the things we have in common through Christ. For adults, fellowship may occur in worship, in Bible study, in serving God together, as well as in socials or specific "fellowship" activities. But young people will probably see fellowship as having fun with other young people. In fact,

they need this type of fellowship. They need to be able to have a good time with Christians so they can see that they don't have to be with people who pull them away from God in order to have fun. You will need to meet them where they are in their thinking in order to encourage them to expand their perspectives. They will eventually come to see that fellowship includes sharing and caring about one another. They will see how fellowship with other Christians of all ages can strengthen them and keep them on the right track spiritually; and how it can provide encouragement and help in time of need. Christians should not try to grow in isolation.

As young people make the effort to grow by doing the things that encourage growth, they open the doors for God to work in their lives with the supernatural power that only He possesses.

Be supportive and encouraging toward your young people. Expect them to do their best, but don't demand more than they are capable of. Many junior highers are still youngsters trapped in a body that is rapidly becoming adult. Your patience, love and encouragement will help stimulate growth better than a hundred lessons.

SESSION PLAN

BEFORE CLASS BEGINS: Obtain the special materials required by the ATTENTION GRABBER.

Attention Grabber

ATTENTION GRABBER (5-10 minutes)

Materials needed: A plant in a pot with soil, a small bag of plant food or fertilizer, a box of snail poison or other pesticide or weed killer, flashlight, bottle of water, and an inflated balloon. Place

everything in view at the front of the classroom.

As you hold up each object, ask students how each would help the potted plant to grow. (Nourishment is provided by soil, water, fertilizer, light—as represented by the flashlight—and air—as represented by the air in the balloon. The pesticide protects the plant from harm.)

Tell students, **Our session today deals with Christian growth. We have looked at several items that help a plant to grow. Now let's look** at some things that cause a Christian to grow spiritually. Only Christians—people who have rooted their lives in Christ—can grow. Remember: no life, no growth. Break off the stem of the plant to drive your point home.

Bible Exploration

EXPLORATION (20-30 minutes)

Step 1 (10-15 minutes): Say, **Turn to your Treasure Seeker worksheet and find the section titled "Acme Grow a Christian." List five things that help a Christian to grow and mature. Look up the Bible verses to find the answers.**

Let students work independently or with a partner. Then ask them to share some of the answers; write their answers on the chalkboard. Guide a discussion by asking the following questions.

Students should mention Bible study as needed for growth. You might ask, **What would you compare the Bible with in the things that are essential for the growth of a plant?** They might give answers such as water, light, or food.

Ask, **In what way is the Bible like the water for a plant? How often should we provide that nourishment for our spiritual life? Why shouldn't we wait until our Christian life starts to droop before we water it?**

Bible memory should also be mentioned. Ask, **What does memorizing parts of the Bible do for you that studying it does not do? How can memorizing verses help keep you from sinning? How can Scripture help you decide right and wrong?**

When your students mention prayer, ask, **What is prayer? When should you pray? What should you pray about?**

Confession of sins should be mentioned. Ask, **Why is it important to confess your sins? What happens if you don't confess them? Can you have close fellowship with God when you have unconfessed sin in your life? What does God do when you confess?**

Students should mention fellowship. Ask, **Why is it important to have Christian friends? What do Christians have to offer that others don't? Is it possible to have an exciting life and not hang around with people who would pull you away from God?**

Step 2 (10-15 minutes): **Look at the "Bugs" part of the Treasure Seeker. Every plant has certain "bugs" that try to keep it from growing. Think about some of the things in your life that keep young people from growing in Christ. These might be things that are good or neutral in themselves, but that can distract people from growing in Christ, such as too much TV watching or spending a lot of time with the wrong crowd. Or they may be things that are bad in themselves, such as sin. Write them on the "bugs" on the page—and you can draw some more "bugs" of your own if you wish.**

Allow students to work. Then regain their attention and discuss their "bugs." Have them tell why or how one or two of their "bugs" can keep a person from growing. Remember that later lessons

Is 59: 1-2

Your students may wish to see this solution to the Fun Page puzzle.

(If you like, write the solution on an extra copy of the Fun Page and pin it to your classroom bulletin board.)

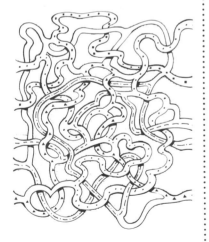

NOTE: The next session requires copies of the *NASB* or *NIV* Bibles. See page 59 for details.

will come back to various aspects of Christian growth, so it is not necessary to cover every detail today in the time available.

OPTIONAL ALTERNATIVE TO *STEP 2* (10 minutes)

Gather students into groups of three or four, and seat each group at a table. Distribute felt markers and illustration boards. Instruct groups to draw a large bug of their own design—the uglier the better—and to label it with a sin or practice which would tend to prevent a junior high Christian's growth. If students wish, allow them to draw something that would help a Christian to grow. When groups are through, ask them to share their thoughts and drawings with the class.

Conclusion and Decision

CONCLUSION (5 minutes)

Tell students, **I want you to work individually on the "Food to Grow On" section of your worksheet. When you are finished, silently ask God to help you with your commitment.**

SUGGESTION: Describe to your students how at least one of these ingredients for Christian growth has been especially meaningful to you.

Close in prayer and distribute the Fun Page take-home paper.

Bugs That Keep Us from Growing

Every plant has "bugs" that keep it from growing. So do Christians. Many things can attack our Christian life to prevent us from growing as we should. On the little bugs below, write the names of things that could prevent growth in a Christian's life. These could be sins of one kind or another, or things that keep us too occupied to grow as we should.

ACME
Grow a Christian Miracle Food

CONGRATULATIONS!

You are the proud owner of one healthy Christian life.

Please feed and care for your Christian life by following the important instructions in the Bible verses below. List five ingredients for growth found in these verses:

2 Timothy 3:16

Psalm 119:11

Luke 18:1

1 John 1:9

Acts 2:42-47 and 1 John 1:7

Food to Grow On

Think back over the actions that contribute to Christian growth that we discussed today—Bible study, Bible memorization, prayer, telling God about your sins and fellowship. Decide which one you need the most work on and determine one thing you will do this week to improve in that area. For example, if you need to start studying your Bible, you might decide that you will spend at least five minutes each day reading God's Word.

I will work on:

The thing I will do to improve:

I will start:

FIVE THE HARD WAY!

Here's a challenge that will test your "mazing" abilities—it's tougher than it looks. Connect each of the "Five Smart Ideas" on the left side of the page to the matching Bible verses on the right by drawing lines along the correct paths through the maze (the numbers on the left match the same numbers on the right). The hard part: You can never cross your path (except on pathways that cross over or under) and you cannot use the same section of pathway twice.

There may be more than one solution.

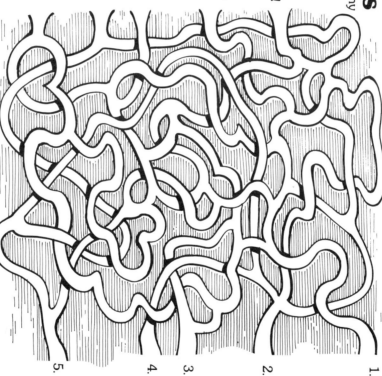

1. "All Scripture is God-breathed and is useful for teaching, rebuking, correcting and training in righteousness."
2 Timothy 3:16

2. "I have hidden your word in my heart that I might not sin against you."
Psalm 119:11

3. "Pray continually."
1 Thessalonians 5:17

4. "If we confess our sins, he is faithful and just and will forgive us our sins and purify us from all unrighteousness."
1 John 1:9

5. "They devoted themselves to the apostles' teaching and to the fellowship, to the breaking of bread and to prayer."
Acts 2:42

FIVE SMART IDEAS

to make you a strong and healthy Christian

1. **Read the Bible— it's God's wisdom for you!**

2. **Memorize God's advice— it'll change your life!**

3. **Pray—talk and listen!**

4. **Apologize to God about your sins—you'll lead a good life!**

5. **Fellowship—build your friendships with fellow believers!**

DAILY NUGGETS

Wisdom from God's Word for you to read each day.

Day 1 Read Psalm 1:1-3. What does the blessed person do?

Day 2 Psalm 1:1-3. What does the blessed person not do? What is the result?

Day 3 Psalm 5:3. What is the writer's attitude after praying?

Day 4 Proverbs 3:5,6. What is an area of your life in which you need "straight paths"?

Day 5 Hebrews 10:24,25. How have other Christians helped you grow in Christ?

Day 6 Philippians 4:8. Try this kind of "right thinking" for a day and see what a difference it makes in your life.

Commit this one to memory, and commit yourself to living it.

"So then, just as you received Christ Jesus as Lord, continue to live in him."

Colossians 2:6

THEME: Five ingredients for Christian growth: Bible study, Bible memorization, prayer, confession, and fellowship.

BIBLE STUDY OUTLINE:

Begin your message by relating the Parable of the Sower found in Luke 8:4-15. Cover these points as time allows:

- The seed represents the Word of God (see verse 11). The Word of God is His message to us. It is truth, it is the light for successful Christian living. It has the power to change hearts and lives.
- The dirt path had become hard from the pounding of traffic. A hard heart can prevent God's message from taking effect.
- Many people are like the rocky soil: they are shallow, with no real depth of Christian character. Soon they are gone.
- Some people are caught in the "thorns" of the day-to-day rat race. Too much time for things, not enough time for God.
- But a person whose heart is receptive to God will grow and mature and lead a productive life; verses 8 and 15 promise that.

NOTES

OBJECT LESSON: THE HEART

Preparation: It is possible to buy a beef heart at most major grocery stores (you may have to ask the butcher). Buy a heart and wrap it in clear plastic food wrap. Refrigerate it until you are ready for the meeting. Keep it concealed in a paper sack until you finish the Bible Study Outline.

As you discuss the nature of the human heart, pass around the beef heart (still in the plastic wrap) for your listeners to handle. Be sure to maintain control of the situation at all times. Your discussion should include the impact of having a cold, hard heart, and the need to have a soft, receptive heart for God. Return the heart to the sack and place it out of sight, then lead a discussion based on the following questions.

DISCUSSION QUESTIONS

1. **How can you tell when a person your age has a hard heart?**
2. **What are some of the things we can do to be softhearted and receptive to God? Coming to hear God's Word like you have tonight is one way. What are some others? [Personal Bible study, memorization, prayer, confession, fellowship: go over each of these in detail.]**
3. **What do you think Jesus meant when He spoke of producing an abundant crop (verses 8 and 15)?**
4. **If "producing an abundant crop" means having an important impact on our world, what are a few things Christians your age could do to be growing such a crop—at home, in school, here at church?**

THE COMPLETE JUNIOR HIGH
BIBLE STUDY RESOURCE
BOOK #1

Some people have hard hearts. But the grace of God can easily shatter that heart and make it soft toward Him. Here are some games that make use of another easily broken object: the egg.

"EGG TOSS"

This is the good old standby. Gather your students into pairs. Each pair is given an egg to toss back and forth, as shown.

Every time the players successfully toss their egg, they are to widen the gap between them by each taking one step backward. Pairs that drop their egg are eliminated. The last remaining pair wins.

You may find that forming two or three teams of several pairs each is more exciting: as one pair from each team competes, the other pairs can cheer until it is their turn.

"EGG EXPRESS"

Have your students take their shoes off and lie on their backs, forming two single file lines as shown.

Using only their feet, players are to pass one egg down the line and back again. First team to finish is the winner. If an egg breaks, the team must start over with a new egg at the beginning of the line.

"SCRAMBLED EGGS"

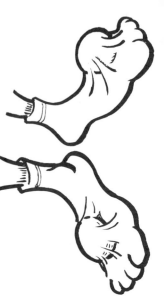

Materials required: A pair of old socks for every player and, of course, lots of eggs.

Have all players remove their shoes and socks. Tell them to wear the socks you provide, with the eggs carefully positioned as illustrated.

Mark a large circle or square on the floor (with rope, tape or chalk) to serve as an out-of-bounds line. Gather all students into the playing field. At the signal, each player is supposed to stomp the other players' eggs to pieces, while protecting his or her own. Only feet can be used, hands must be kept away from other players. The last surviving egg belongs to the winner. You will probably find it takes several sharp-eyed sponsors to spot the longest-lived egg, as it will probably be crushed before the players come to a halt.

Bible Study

WHAT THE SESSION IS ABOUT

Reading God's Word is important to a Christian's spiritual growth and vitality.

SCRIPTURE STUDIED

Psalm 33:20; Jeremiah 23:29; John 20:31; Romans 1:16; Colossians 1:5; 2 Timothy 3:16; Hebrews 4:12.

KEY PASSAGE

"Consequently, faith comes from hearing the message, and the message is heard through the word of Christ." Romans 10:17

AIMS OF THE SESSION

During this session your learners will:

1. Recognize the Bible as the source of knowledge about God.
2. Tell the benefits people today receive from reading the Bible.
3. Commit themselves to a regular Bible reading schedule for the coming week.

INSIGHTS FOR THE LEADER

In Session 4 we studied key ingredients necessary for spiritual growth: Bible study, Bible memorization, prayer, confession, and fellowship. Today we will take a closer look at Bible study. This session will introduce your students to some of the benefits of reading the Bible.

The next session, Session 6, also deals with God's Word; it will introduce your students to Bible study tools and methods that will help them better understand the Scriptures. These two lessons together should help get learners interested in the Bible and demonstrate to them that God's book is something they can understand and profit from.

In this session, students will find that the Bible is **"useful for teaching, rebuking, correcting and training in righteousness"** (2 Tim. 3:16). Through His Word, God teaches His people how He wants them to live. When they sin, the Word brings a warning. When they make mistakes, it shows them the right path to which they need to return. It shows them God's righteousness and tells them how they can experience righteousness (right standing before God) in their lives.

The Bible is a tool in God's hand. It is **"like a hammer which shatters a rock"** (Jer. 23:29, NASB). God's Word is the truth; when it comes up against falsehood, Scripture shatters it.

The Word of God is **"living and active"** (Heb. 4:12). It is alive. It produces change in people's lives. It penetrates deeply; it **"judges the thoughts and attitudes of the heart"** (v. 12). There is no place to hide from the truths God reveals in His Word. When young people let God's Word into their minds and hearts, the Word will show what is right and what is wrong in their thoughts and attitudes. God wants His people to be righteous inside and out. Right thoughts and attitudes lead to right actions, while sinful thoughts and attitudes lead to sinful actions.

The Bible was written for a specific purpose: **"That you may believe that Jesus is the Christ, the Son of God, and that by believing you may have life in his name"** (John 20:31). God wants people to know about the gift of salvation He offers to them through His Son. That's why He provides the Bible. It gives all the information a person needs in order to obtain eternal life.

God's Word is the good news, the gospel, which is **"the power of God for the salvation of everyone who believes"** (Rom. 1:16). We need God's Word to tell us about the salvation He offers.

God's Word is **a consuming fire** (see Jer. 5:14). It judges our thoughts and motives, and thus helps us live more godly lives.

Another metaphor is that God's Word is **the sword of the Spirit** (see Eph. 6:17). As in Hebrews 4:12, this image depicts the cut-

NOTES

ting, penetrating power of the message. It is the Christian's weapon of attack against all the pressures that seek to destroy spiritual life. It cuts through pretense and hypocrisy and reveals the truth.

The Bible is **"the word of truth"** (Col. 1:5). It tells us about God, about ourselves, and about the world around us. We can be confident of the Bible because it is true.

God's Word is **a lamp and a light** (see Ps. 119:105). It shows us the right way to go and reveals the obstacles that might make us stumble. If students have ever walked down a dark road at night, they know that it is scary. They never know when they will stumble over a rock, run into a tree, or twist their ankles in a hole. Light makes everything clear and enables a person to walk confidently. God's Word sheds light for the Christian's walk through life.

God provides **guidance** through His Word (see Isa. 58:11). He wants to help Christians lead the best possible lives, and so He gives them His instructions in His Word.

When Christians need help, they can turn to the Word to find out about God, who is **"our help and our shield"** (Ps. 33:20). The Word helps believers by revealing God, showing His power and His love. It shows His desire and His ability to help, protect, and comfort His children. It also shows Christians how to live for Him and how to experience His power in daily living.

During this session you will guide your students in examining these benefits of reading and studying God's Word. A major factor which will influence them to want to gain these benefits will be your own honest sharing of the ways the Bible has been helpful to you in recent weeks. Then your students will be likely to make the Bible a part of their daily lives, and they will discover many more benefits for themselves.

SESSION PLAN

BEFORE CLASS BEGINS: To best perform the EXPLORATION activity, your students will need copies of the NASB or NIV Bibles.

Attention Grabber

ATTENTION GRABBER (5-7 minutes)

Tell students, **Turn to the "What's It Good For?" section of the Treasure Seeker worksheet and try to guess the purposes of the antique objects.**

Let students work individually or in pairs for a few minutes. Then ask for volunteers to share their answers. (In order: cherry stoner, wooden whistle, table lamp, burglar alarm, spittoon, potato peeler.)

Focus attention on the purpose of the session by saying something like this: **It has been fun trying to figure out what some of these old objects were good for. Now let's think about what the Bible is good for. What do you think the purpose of the Bible is?**

Allow students to respond. The key answer you are looking for is that the Bible is a source of knowledge about God and a guide for living according to God's plan. Respond positively to all students who participate, even if they do not give the exact answer you are seeking. You might say something like this: **The Bible does have many different purposes. Can you think of one that would be even more important than those suggested so far?** Then explain, **In our session today, we're going to be looking at some of the benefits of reading and studying the Bible.**

SUGGESTION: Instead of using the antique objects on the Treasure Seeker, bring a box containing several odd items that students will not immediately recognize. Search for items such as a buttonhook, a garlic press, or unusual tools. Make sure these are not too easy to guess, or the activity will seem childish.

Bible Exploration

EXPLORATION (20-30 minutes)

Materials needed: Several copies of the *New American Standard Bible* (NASB) and/or the *New International Version* (NIV).

Step 1 (10-15 minutes): **Turn to the crossword puzzle on your worksheet. Work in pairs to complete the puzzle according to the directions you find there. The words in the puzzle are based, whenever possible, on the *New American Standard Bible* (NASB) or the *New International Version* (NIV).**

Step 2 (10-15 minutes): When students have completed the puzzle, ask for volunteers to share answers. As they describe the various benefits of reading the Bible, draw out life applications by asking questions such as these: **In what ways do Christians need correction from God's Word? How does the Bible help you when you make a mistake? What are some false things in a person's life that the Word might expose? What are some changes that might occur in a junior higher's life when the Word is living**

and active for that person? **Why does God care about a person's thoughts and attitudes? How can a person know what to believe about God or Christ?**

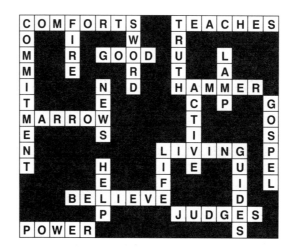

If you cannot locate enough *NASB* or *NIV* Bibles for this Exploration activity, read the proper verses aloud from your copy as students work.

NOTES

NOTE: For the next session, you'll need to gather several Bible reference books. See page 71 for details. Also see page 70 for other materials required.

OPTIONAL ALTERNATIVE TO *STEP 2*:

Design an ad to persuade people to read the Bible. The Bible refers to itself as a sword. You might design an ad showing how it can cut through false teaching. Here's how to get started: (1) Think about the people at whom your ad is aimed. Direct it to people who do not read the Bible, but would do so if they had a good reason to. (2) Think about ways the benefits you have studied today would appeal to your target audience. Pick one or two of those benefits to use in your ad. (3) Decide on the wording and the design or art you want to have in your ad, and get it all down on paper.

While students work, make comments and ask questions to stimulate their thoughts. Refer to the questions in the original *Step 2* for ideas.

Ask volunteers to display their ads and explain the benefits of reading the Bible that they chose to emphasize in their ads.

Conclusion and Decision

CONCLUSION (5-10 minutes)

Your final assignment is to design a book cover for your Bible to remind you to read it each day this week. Take the butcher paper and the felt pens and make an attractive design that says "Read Me" or something similar. Somewhere on the cover—perhaps on an inside flap—draw boxes for each day of the week and label them Monday, Tuesday, Wednesday, etc. Then you can check off the boxes as you read from the Scripture each day. As you read, watch for the benefits that we discovered during this session.

Since daily Bible study should also include prayer, you might want to encourage your students to begin a prayer list to remind them of people for whom to pray.

Close in prayer and distribute the Fun Page take-home paper.

Treasure Seeker

SESSION 5

What's It Good For?

These items were used around the turn of the century. We know you weren't around then, but can you figure out what these contraptions are or what they are used for?

1.

2.

3.

4.

KITCH | DIN R'HALL | PARL | LIBR | 2'FL

PARTRICK & CARTER
PHILADELPHIA.

5.

6.

Try This Crossword Puzzle!

ACROSS

1. When we are really sad and low, God's Word _____ us.
4. According to 2 Timothy 3:16, God's word _____ us.
5. God's Word is sometimes referred to as the "_____ Book."
8. Jeremiah 23:29 says God's Word is like this tool.
11. Hebrews 4:12 says God's Word is so powerful it penetrates through the bone and into this substance.
12. Hebrews 4:12 describes God's Word as "active" and _____.
15. God's Word is first written so that all will _____. (John 20:31)
16. God's Word also _____ our thoughts and attitudes. (Heb. 4:12)
17. God's Word gives _____ for the salvation of everyone who believes. (Rom. 1:16)

DOWN

1. An agreement or pledge to read God's Word in the future is a _____.
2. Jeremiah 5:14 tells us that God's Word is like a consuming _____.
3. In Ephesians 6:17 Paul tells early Christians to use God's Word like this tool.
4. God tells us that we can be confident that everything in the Bible is the _____ and helpful for our spiritual growth. (Col. 1:5)
6. Psalm 119:105 tells us that the Bible is a _____ and a light for our daily walk with Christ.
7. The gospel message of God's Word is often called the Good _____.
9. Hebrews 4:12 describes God's Word using this word that means moving and energetic.
10. The message or _____ of Jesus Christ is fully contained in God's Word.
12. According to John 20:31, God's Word contains all the information we need in order to know how to have eternal _____ .
13. When we read God's Word it _____ and directs our daily life. (Isa. 58:11)
14. In times of trouble we can read God's Word for _____. (Ps. 33:20)

UH, OH! WE BROKE IT!

Why did God cause the Bible to be written to us? Good question! And the answer is in this word/picture game. Just one problem: we broke it. The first part is OK, but it is up to you to fix the rest of the game by placing the pictures at the bottom into the proper spaces in the game. Don't get the wrong combination or who knows what weird answer you'll find! This is a very tough game, so be patient. The solution is printed upside down at the bottom of the page.

 – ter

3 – re + se ARE wr + 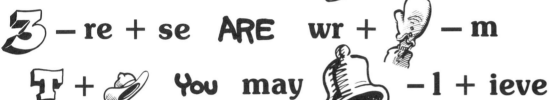 – m

T + 🎩 You may 🔔 – l + ieve

t + ... Jesus .... – h the ....

– imney + r + ... – f, the ....

– ap + n of .... – l, and that by

.... – e + ... – d + eving, ...

may have .... – cf + e in his

.... – il + me.

DAILY NUGGETS

Day 1 Read Matthew 4:4. You need food to keep your body alive. What do you suppose happens to your spiritual life if you don't feed it daily with God's Word?

Day 2 Psalm 119:18. Have you asked God to show you wonderful things from His Word?

Day 3 Psalm 1:2,3. Have you been feeling like a well-watered, healthy tree? If not, check how much time you spend in God's Word.

Day 4 1 Peter 2:2,3. How does milk help babies? How does God's Word help you?

Day 5 Joshua 1:8. Write out this verse in your own words.

Day 6 Acts 17:10,11. When you hear sermons and other Bible teaching, do you check it out in the Word for yourself?

HOT THOT

"Consequently, faith comes from hearing the message, and the message is heard through the word of Christ."
Romans 10:17

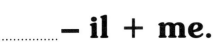    

SOLUTION: "But these [things Jesus did] are written that you may believe that Jesus is the Christ, the Son of God, and that by believing you may have life in his name." (John 20:31.)

POP SHEET

THEME: The Bible shows us how to remain safe in an evil world.

BIBLE STUDY OUTLINE:

Read Ephesians 6:10-18 to (or with) your students, making these points as time allows:

- We live in a satanic world and, as Christians, are caught in a struggle against Satan. In fact, becoming a Christian doesn't make living easier, it often makes it *harder* because we enter into the realm of the supernatural.
- Only God has the strength to stand against Satan. Therefore we, if we want to survive, must always look to Him for power and protection.
- God has given us a "suit of armor" to wear as protection. (At this point, refer to the OBJECT LESSON.)

DISCUSSION QUESTIONS

1. **Do you believe that demons are "alive and well" and working in the world today? Why or why not?**
2. **Can you think of things that Satan would tend to use to "wipe out" people your age?**
3. **How can you know when an action or attitude is wrong or satanic? (Judge it against God's Word.)**
4. **If God's Word is our guide, and evil really is rampant in our world, does this give us strong motivation to know and obey the Bible?**

You may wish to conclude the lesson by offering to supply easy-to-read Bibles to those who have need, and by assigning a passage for students to "tackle" on their own, such as 1 John 1:9 or the third chapter of John.

OBJECT LESSON:
THE CHRISTIAN'S ARMOR

Borrow a football uniform (the kind worn for American football) from a student or from the local high school. As you speak, demonstrate the various parts of the uniform:

Verse 14: *The belt of truth.* Show your listeners the pants, hip and knee pads, even the athletic supporter. Speak on the subject of *truth;* i.e., that any Christian who tends to stray from the truth (the Bible) is unprotected in the spiritual battle.

The breastplate of righteousness. Hold up the shoulder pads, and tell listeners that a life lived the way God wants it to be lived is essential to Christian survival.

Verse 15: The *feet;* the *gospel of peace.* Let your students handle the shoes. The gospel is the good news of salvation which brings peace between the Christian and God.

Verse 16: The *shield of faith.* Demonstrate the forearm pads and elbow pads which serve to deflect the blows of the opposition. Point out that just as football players must have faith in their coach, Christians must trust and obey the Lord.

Verse 17: The *helmet of salvation.* Perhaps the most important part of all.

Say something like, **A person would have to be a fool to play football with no protective uniform. In the same way, a Christian cannot hope to do well in the struggle against evil unless he or she puts on the armor of God.**

Now point out that, unlike the football's uniform, the Christian's armor does have offensive weapons. The *sword of the Spirit* is the Bible. Ask students to imagine the damage a football team armed with swords could cause! Tell them that a Christian who knows and follows the Bible can do real damage to Satan's plans.

The second weapon is *prayer* (see verse 18). A Christian who wears the protection described in this passage and who wields the weapons of God's Word and prayer is undefeatable.

THE COMPLETE JUNIOR HIGH
BIBLE STUDY RESOURCE
BOOK #1

If you want to add a little impact to the idea of spiritual warfare, try some of these fun "war games."

"MINI DYE WAR"

Give each player a white T-shirt with a small target on the back. Place everyone inside a large boundary (a circle or square indicated with rope, hose, tape or chalk). Distribute squirt guns filled with watered-down food coloring. (When you dilute the dye, add sufficient water so that the mixture will be strong enough to just slightly stain your skin.)

On the signal, players are to "zap" the targets of as many other players as possible, while trying to avoid being "zapped." Call a halt after a couple of minutes and compare targets to see who has the cleanest target. Be sure to collect squirt guns.

"LITTLE JOHN"

Place a six-foot 2x4 on two sturdy chairs, as shown. Two students attempt to knock each other off with rolled-up newspaper bats or padded sticks.

"TOSS OUT"

Boys lock arms as illustrated, girls try to toss boys out of the circle. Last boys remaining are winners.
Tip: Tell girls to work together on just one or two boys at a time.

"DUELING BALLOONS"

Two players face each other, standing about six feet apart on marks made with tape. At a signal, each quickly blows up a balloon and lets it go. If a flying balloon hits a player, that player loses. If no one is hit, the players keep trying as quickly as they can, each time shooting from the marks. Several duels can be going on at the same time.

How to Use the Bible SESSION 6

INSIGHTS FOR THE LEADER

WHAT THE SESSION IS ABOUT

Bible study helps and methods which will make the Bible come alive.

SCRIPTURE STUDIED

John 6:63; Hebrews 4:12,13.

KEY PASSAGE

"Do your best to present yourself to God as one approved, a workman who does not need to be ashamed and who correctly handles the word of truth." 2 Timothy 2:15

AIMS OF THE SESSION

During this session your learners will:
1. Examine barriers to understanding the Bible.
2. Become familiar with simple Bible study tools and methods.
3. Experience a selected plan for discovery in God's Word.

Many young people do not read the Bible much because they think it is extremely difficult to understand, that it's boring, or that it's something you get into when you grow up. These ideas may come from trying to study difficult books of the Bible without adequate help; from using Bible versions written in archaic language; or from previous boring Bible study meetings. Also, junior highers are just beginning to grasp abstracts, and much of the biblical message is abstract.

Another reason young people do not read the Bible is simply that they do not give it a high priority in their life. They expect to function on what they receive on Sunday. (That's like expecting to live on one meal a week.)

Bible study tools, as introduced in this session, will help those who are interested in reading the Bible. But they cannot solve motivational problems. The easiest version of the Bible still won't appeal to a junior higher who does not see any value in reading Scripture. But for young people who do see value in the Bible, today's session will provide an introduction to some simple tools that will help them better understand God's Word and realize its applicability to their lives. The Bible study tools are identified and their functions are described in the first Bible exploration activity.

Then students are invited to apply what they have learned in the session to Hebrews 4:12,13, which is printed in the Treasure Seeker worksheet. This passage says, "The Word of God is living and active. Sharper than any double-edged sword, it penetrates even to dividing soul and spirit, joints and marrow; it judges the thoughts and attitudes of the heart. Nothing in all creation is hidden from God's sight. Everything is uncovered and laid bare before the eyes of him to whom we must give account."

God's Word is living and active. It is not merely an interesting book; it has power to change people's lives. Jesus said, "The Spirit gives life; the flesh counts for nothing. The words I have spoken to you are spirit and they are life" (John 6:63). God's Word gives us new life—spiritual life.

The Word is also like a **double-edged sword.** It penetrates into the deepest parts of a person and reveals what is there of good and evil. Many Christians can testify to this power. As they read the Word, they find the Lord rebuking them for certain attitudes or desires or actions. When they confess and agree with God that they have been wrong, He brings cleansing and healing and comfort, assuring them through the Word that they are forgiven.

The Scripture also points out that **God knows everything.** People sometimes think they can hide bad attitudes and selfish motives from God and satisfy Him with actions that seem outwardly acceptable. But God isn't fooled. He knows every thought we think,

NOTES

every motive, every attitude. This verse gives an answer to young people who might ask, "Should we confess to God everything about our inner thoughts and feelings?" The answer is yes, since He knows all about those thoughts and feelings and will hold His people accountable for them.

This study has provided a brief examination of the Scripture in Hebrews. It has not been intended as an exhaustive treatment. Many questions your learners will have can be answered by the simple Bible study tools suggested in the session. Encourage them to use the tools so that they can study and understand God's Word on their own.

SESSION PLAN

BEFORE CLASS BEGINS: Gather the materials required by the EXPLORATION and, if necessary, the CREATIVE OPTION below.

Attention Grabber

ATTENTION GRABBER (5-10 minutes)

Instruct students to work individually or in pairs to solve the "Translator" section of the Treasure Seeker.

When they are finished, regain students' attention and let them tell their translations of the sayings. The correct versions are as follows:

> Mary had a little lamb,
> Its fleece was white as snow;
> Everywhere that Mary went
> The lamb was sure to go.

> An apple a day keeps the doctor away.

> The quick brown fox
> jumped over the lazy dog.

Lead a brief discussion by saying something like this: **You've probably been frustrated trying to figure out all these sayings. Many of you probably feel the same sort of frustration when you try to read your Bibles. What makes it hard to understand the Bible? What do you think would help you understand it better?** (Let students respond.)

Make a transition to the next part of the session by commenting, **We're going to discover some simple tools and methods that will help you understand the Bible.**

CREATIVE OPTION (5-10 minutes)

Materials needed: Several books and magazines, each aimed at different levels of reading ability. For example: a young child's storybook, a comic book, a teenage romance novel or mystery, science or science fiction magazine, cookbook, auto repair manual, Bible, college textbook, computer manual.

List the title of each item on the chalkboard or overhead projector. Hold up each book or magazine in turn and briefly describe each one. Tell your students that you want them to vote for the two or three they think would be the hardest to understand. Ask for a show of hands and write the number of votes under each title.

The Bible will probably rate as a difficult book. Tell your students that you understand their frustration, and that the purpose of this session is to show them some good ways to make the Bible much easier to understand and enjoy.

SUGGESTION: As students vote, discuss with them some reasons why they might not want to read the various books and magazines. Answers will probably include: *too long, looks dull,* and *too hard to read.* When you focus in on the Bible, tell students that you once felt that way yourself about God's Word. But now you have learned some Bible study "secrets" that you are going to share with them.

Bible Exploration

EXPLORATION (25-35 minutes)

Materials needed: As many of these Bible study tools as you can obtain: easy-to-read Bible version; Bible concordance; Bible with cross-references; Bible dictionary; English dictionary; colored pencils; copies of the "Bible Study Chart" that you will find in the "Clip Art and Other Goodies" section at the end of this book; copies of "Bible Study Tools" Teaching Resource Page.

You also need a hat or other container and the "Name that Tool" Teaching Resource Page (prepared as described on the page's instructions).

Step 1 (10-12 minutes): Display all the Bible study tools you have obtained. Explain *all* the tools mentioned, showing the ones you have brought as you come to them.

There are some simple tools that will help you a great deal when you read and study the Bible. The *easy-to-read Bible version* will often clarify problems immediately. It uses up-to-date language and simpler words to help you understand the Bible's meaning. Have students compare 2 Timothy 2:15 in two or three versions.

***The Bible concordance* is an alphabetical index of the words in the Bible. Most show the immediate context of the word so you can get some idea of what the passage is about. Some concordances list all the references where every word is found. Abridged concordances list only the most important words and only the most important instances of each word. Many concordances are based on the *King James Version;* others are based on various recent translations. Many Bibles have a limited concordance in the back; these can be helpful in finding verses or making studies of biblical subjects. Concordances enable a person to study subjects or words**

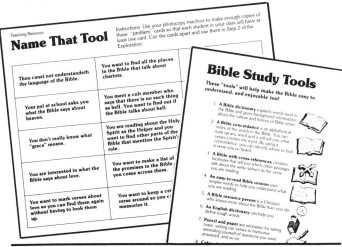

NOTES

and to make comparisons. Have a student look up a word such as "truth" in a concordance and read one or two entries.

A Bible with cross-references **helps in this way; when you are reading a certain passage, and you want to know what else the Bible says about the ideas in the passage, you can look at the cross-references and they will lead you to other verses on the same subject.** Have a student look up 2 Timothy 2:15, find a cross-reference, and look up and read aloud one verse listed.

A Bible dictionary **explains words used in the Bible and gives historical and cultural information. It may also explain something of why and when they were written.** Have a student look up "Timothy" in a Bible dictionary and read the first paragraph of the definition. (Read the paragraph ahead of time; if there are difficult words in it, be prepared to help the student with them.)

An English dictionary **gives definitions of words and may help you understand terms used in the Bible that you are not familiar with.** Have a student look up the word "approved" in an English dictionary and read the definition.

Pencil and paper **are useful for taking notes, making lists, writing out verses to remember, keeping track of what you are reading, and so on.** *Colored pencils* **can be used to mark verses you want to find again easily. You can use different colors for different general topics. For example, you might mark everything about faith in green.**

I also have some copies of this "Bible Study Chart" which I will hand out to you in a few moments. It has helpful features that will guide you as you study your Bible.

A "Bible resource person" **is a Christian who is older and who knows more about the Bible than a junior higher. This might be a parent, pastor, Sunday School teacher, youth leader, or some other knowledgeable person.**

Step 2 (10-12 minutes): Distribute copies of "Bible Study Tools" from the Teaching Resource page. Put the "Name That Tool" cards with "problems" into the hat or container. Explain to students, **I'm going to allow you an opportunity to select one card from the hat. After you have read the problem on the card, decide which Bible study tool will help you solve the problem.**

Distribute the problem cards and let each student read the problems and explain which Bible study tool he or she would use to solve each problem. If you have more cards than students, go around a second time until all the cards are drawn. If you have too many students, prepare in advance by making up extra cards, repeating some of the problems or including some new ones of your own.

Following are the problems along with suggestions for the tools to use.

Thou canst not understandeth the language of the Bible. Try reading an easier version or a paraphrase. There are a number of translations and paraphrases which will enable junior high readers to grasp God's message.

Your pal at school asks you what the Bible says about heaven. This is a good problem to take to a Bible dictionary or to a "Bible resource person" who can direct the learner to appropriate Scriptures dealing with the topic.

You don't really know what "grace" means. Word definitions are found in dictionaries. An English dictionary will give a general explanation of what the word means; sometimes this is enough to clarify a verse. The Bible dictionary defines the word, and may tell about special ways it is used in the Bible or the special meaning it has to Christians.

You are interested in what the Bible says about love. A concordance will help here. A young person can look up the word "love" and find the verses that use this word. A Bible resource person might also help.

You want to mark verses about love so you can find them again without having to look them up. Mark them with a colored pencil and they will stand out when you turn the pages.

You meet a cult member who says that there is no such thing as hell. You want to find out if the Bible talks about hell. Look it up in a concordance or ask a resource person.

You are reading about the Holy Spirit as the Helper and you want to find other parts of the Bible that mention Him in this role. A Bible with cross-references will help. Cross-references lead to other verses dealing with the same topic. A concordance will also help.

You want to make a list of all the promises in the Bible as you come across them. Paper and pencil will help here.

You want to keep a certain verse around so you can memorize it. Use paper and pencil; write it down and carry it with you.

You want to learn why Paul wrote Galatians. Look in a Bible dictionary under "Galatians" and under "Paul." A Bible resource person might also help.

You want to find out what Bible verses to look up to help you witness. Ask a Bible resource person for guidance.

You are reading about the Crucifixion in Matthew, and you want to find out what the other three Gospels say about it. A cross-reference Bible should list the locations of the Crucifixion accounts in the other Gospels.

You keep getting stuck on words you don't understand; you would like to be able to read the Bible without having to stop to look up words. An easy-language version should keep you going.

You want to mark verses dealing with salvation so you can find them quickly in your Bible. Mark them with colored pencils.

You want to find all the places in the Bible that talk about chariots. Look in a concordance under "chariot(s)."

Step 3 (5-10 minutes): Say something like this: **Now that we have an idea of some of the tools available to help you in your Bible study, I want you to have the opportunity to experience a brief Bible study on your own. Turn to your Treasure Seeker worksheet and find the "Drain It Dry" section. Working individually, carefully study the instructions so you will understand what you are to do. Then study and mark the Scripture assignment and use the available Bible study tools according to the instructions.**

Move around the room and be available to help students with any questions or problems they may have.

When time is up, spend a few moments talking with your students about what they have experienced. Ask them what they have learned, what problems they had, and whether they are willing to try reading the Bible regularly for another week, using one or more study tools.

Distribute the "Bible Study Charts."

Conclusion and Decision

CONCLUSION (2 minutes)

Explain to students, **You are to write your responses to the following statements: "One thing I learned from the Bible study today . . ." and "One Bible study tool I would like to use more is . . ."**

Offer to help provide Bible study tools to interested students (by showing them how to use the church library or by getting the church to help purchase books for the students).

Close in prayer. Distribute the Fun Page take-home paper. Point out the "Daily Nuggets" section which provides a week's worth of Bible passages to study.

Your students may wish to see this solution to the Fun Page puzzle.

(If you like, write the solution on an extra copy of the Fun Page and pin it to your classroom bulletin board.)

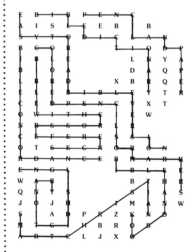

NOTE: The next session requires some extra photocopying. See page 90 for instructions.

Treasure Seeker

SESSION 6

Translator

Here are some strange but familiar poems and sayings that have been made a bit more difficult by using ten-dollar college words.

Try to translate the following "verses" into their original form.

**Mary possessed a miniscule juvenile sheep;
its coiffure was hoary as crystallized ice flakes;
and wheresoever that Mary hied,
the juvenile sheep was obliged to wend.**

A malus a 24 hour period disallows the general practitioner.

The mercurial cordovan vulpes vulpes vaulted athwart the slothful cur.

Drain It Dry

Read the Bible passage printed below. Answer all the questions by using the Bible study tools your teacher provides. It is up to you to decide which tools to apply to each question. (Ask your teacher for assistance if needed.)

"For the word of God is living and active. Sharper than any double-edged sword, it penetrates even to dividing soul and spirit, joints and marrow; it judges the thoughts and attitudes of the heart. Nothing in all creation is hidden from God's sight. Everything is uncovered and laid bare before the eyes of him to whom we must give account."

1. **What does "marrow" mean?**

2. **What does "the word of God" refer to?**

3. **List two other Bible passages which mention the heart.**

4. **Where in the Bible is this passage found?**

5. **Who wrote the book in which this passage is found?**

6. **Write out the passage in a different version.**

Name That Tool

Instructions: Use your photocopy machine to make enough copies of these "problem" cards so that each student in your class will have at least one card. Cut the cards apart and use them in *Step 2* of the Exploration.

Thou canst not understandeth the language of the Bible.	**You want to find all the places in the Bible that talk about chariots.**	**You want to learn why Paul wrote Galatians.**
Your pal at school asks you what the Bible says about heaven.	**You meet a cult member who says that there is no such thing as hell. You want to find out if the Bible talks about hell.**	**You want to find out what Bible verses to look up to help you tell others about Jesus.**
You don't really know what "grace" means.	**You are reading about the Holy Spirit as the Helper and you want to find other parts of the Bible that mention the Spirit's role.**	**You are reading about the Crucifixion in Matthew, and you want to find out what the other three Gospels say about it.**
You are interested in what the Bible says about love.	**You want to make a list of all the promises in the Bible as you come across them.**	**You keep getting stuck on words you don't understand; you would like to be able to read the Bible without having to stop to look up words.**
You want to mark verses about love so you can find them again without having to look them up.	**You want to keep a certain verse around so you can memorize it.**	**You want to mark verses dealing with salvation so you can find them quickly in your Bible.**

Bible Study Tools

These "tools" will help make the Bible easy to understand, and enjoyable too!

1. **A Bible dictionary** explains words used in the Bible and gives background information about the culture and history of Bible times.

2. **A Bible concordance** is an alphabetical index of the words in the Bible. You can look up any word and it will tell you what verses contain the word. By using a concordance, you can identify where to find a verse you've heard.

3. **A Bible with cross-references** contains footnotes that tell you which other passages talk about the same subject as the verse you are reading.

4. **An easy-to-read Bible version** uses simpler words to help you understand what you are reading.

5. **A Bible resource person** is a Christian who knows more about the Bible than you do.

6. **An English dictionary** can help you define tough words.

7. **Pencil and paper** are necessary for taking notes, writing out verses to memorize, reminding yourself of questions you want answered, and so on.

8. **Colored pencils** can be used to mark verses you wish to find again easily. You can use different colors for different general topics. For example, you might mark everything about faith in green.

B IS FOR BIBLE!

FUN page!

If you would like to discover for yourself God's wisdom in the Bible, you'd be smart to get some help from the nine Bible study "tools" listed below. The phrases printed in bold letters can be found in the big B-shaped letter grid. Your job is to find the phrases and circle or shade them. But B warned! The phrases twist and turn all over the place—up, down, sideways, backward, and diagonally.

Bible Study Tools and Helps:

1. **EASY TO READ BIBLE VERSION** (Modern language and simpler words.)

2. **BIBLE CONCORDANCE** (Locates words and verses in the Bible.)

3. **BIBLE WITH CROSS REFERENCES** (Locates other verses on the same subject as the verse you are reading.)

4. **BIBLE DICTIONARY** (Explains words used in the Bible.)

5. **BIBLE HANDBOOK** (Gives a quick overview of Bible history.)

6. **ENGLISH DICTIONARY** (Helps you define words and terms.)

7. **COLORED PENCILS OR MARKERS** (For marking your favorite verses.)

8. **PENCIL AND PAPER** (For recording questions and comments.)

9. **SMART CHRISTIAN** (To answer difficult questions.)

```
E  B  I  B  P  E  N  C
A  I  S  L  E  E  I  B
S  Y  T  O  D  I  C  L  A  N
B  C  O  R  T  I  O  D  P
I  I  B  L  E  L  N  Y  A
B  I  O  A  B  R  Q  P
L  B  R  D  X  B  R  Q  E
E  L  E  I  B  L  E  Y  T  R
C  E  D  P  E  N  C  V  X  T
O  W  I  T  H  C  I  E  W
N  R  S  O  R  L  I  W
C  E  F  E  R  E  S  I
O  T  S  E  C  N  O  R  O  N
R  D  A  N  C  E  B  M  A  R  K
E  N  G  L  I  B  L  E  E
W  A  R  I  B  T  H  R
Q  N  Y  S  S  I  A  S
J  O  J  H  I  M  A  N  W
S  I  A  D  P  R  Z  K  N  D
M  T  C  I  H  B  R  O  B
A  R  T  C  L  J  X  O
```

DAILY NUGGETS

Wisdom from God's Word for you to read each day.

Day 1 Read Psalm 40:8. Start a chart with headings for "God's Law" and "My heart." As you read the Bible day by day, write down under "God's Law" the instructions He gives (for example, "Love your neighbor"). Then, whenever you feel that you are really convinced of the truth and value of the instruction, write it in the "My heart" side of your chart.

Day 2 Psalm 119:11. What is one good reason for having God's Word in your heart, mentioned in this verse?

Day 3 Isaiah 55:10,11. What does God's Word accomplish?

Day 4 John 15:3. Do you need cleaning up inside? Let God's Word do the job.

Day 5 Romans 10:17. Reading God's Word will help improve your what?

Day 6 1 John 1:4,5. Why did John write? God, according to verse 5, is what?

Hot Tip!

"Do your best to present yourself to God as one approved, a workman who does not need to be ashamed and who correctly handles the word of truth."

2 Timothy 2:15

THE COMPLETE JUNIOR HIGH BIBLE STUDY RESOURCE BOOK #1
© 1987 GL/LIGHT FORCE, VENTURA, CA 93006

POP SHEET

THEME: The Bible is our guide to successful living; we must follow it.

BIBLE STUDY OUTLINE:

This study focuses on James 1:22-25, the mirror analogy. As you read this passage to your students, go over the following ideas as time allows:

- James is writing to Christians who were facing tough trials and hardships (as mentioned in James 1:2). In verses 22 to 25, he makes it clear that the Bible is the source of answers and blessing—but only for those who *do* what the Bible says.
- The Bible is like a mirror; it shows us what we are really like and what we need to do. Often, we don't like what it shows us.
- But we are expected to take action and do it!
- Just as it is important to look in a mirror quite often, it is important to take a look in the Bible frequently. Having a Bible by the bedside to read at night is a good habit to get into.

OBJECT LESSON: THE MIRROR

As you give the lesson, hold up a mirror for all to see.

Ask your listeners to imagine themselves jumping out of bed in the morning, looking in the mirror and seeing they are a real mess. Green teeth, "goobers" in the eyes, and hair that looks like palm trees. But instead of doing anything about it, each just heads out to school as if nothing is wrong.

At school, people laugh and tell them they are slobs. "We know," they smile. "The mirror revealed our problems. We look awful!"

Tell your students that it's not likely anyone would go anywhere knowing what the mirror revealed. Yet many times we read something in the Bible and think, *I fall short of this instruction,* and do nothing about it. The Bible reflects the truth like a mirror. Only a fool avoids the truth.

No one expects a mirror to do anything about the way a person looks. The mirror reveals the truth, but it is up to that person to make the needed changes. In the same way, the Bible we are reading today shows us what we are really like and what we need to do—but it is up to us to actually do what it says.

DISCUSSION QUESTIONS

1. **Name some of the things the Bible expects us to be doing as Christians.**
2. **Are these hard for someone your age to do? Why or why not?**
3. **If they are hard, where can a person go to get help?**
4. **James calls the Word of God "law." What is a law, and why do you suppose James uses the word here? How does this law give freedom?**
5. **In verse 25, James says that we will be blessed if we follow the Bible's instructions. What does the word "blessed" mean to someone your age?**

THE COMPLETE JUNIOR HIGH
BIBLE STUDY RESOURCE
BOOK #1

Some games of skill, made more difficult upon reflection.

"DUELING MARSHMALLOWS"

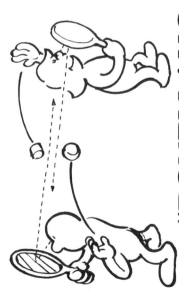

While holding mirrors, two players positioned as shown attempt to hit each other by throwing marshmallows over their shoulders. Players are not allowed to dodge. Several tries may be required before someone is "killed."

You can have winners play winners until a "Fastest Marshmallow in the West" takes all comers.

Marshmallows dipped in flour will leave records of where they land.

"EGNELLAHC ELBIB DRAWKCAB"

For your informal Bible studies, make posters of verses for students to read in a large mirror. First person to correctly read or identify each verse wins.

"MAKING UP IS HARD TO DO"

Three boy volunteers are seated at the front of the group, their good shirts removed or covered. Each boy's face is made up by a girl who can watch what she's doing only by looking in a mirror. Provide red lipstick, eye liner, rouge, hair spray, and so on.

ALSO:

1. A dot-to-dot game or maze can be made tough when the player has to view it in a mirror.

2. Many of the old standby games can be made hilarious by requiring mirrors. Try the one where a kid lies on the floor with a cup in his mouth while another stands on a chair trying to drop ice cream and chocolate into the cup. If the "dropper" uses a mirror, it's likely he'll miss the whole floor!

Prayer

INSIGHTS FOR THE LEADER

WHAT THE SESSION IS ABOUT

Why, where, and when we should pray, and with what attitude.

SCRIPTURE STUDIED

Psalm 5:3; 86:6,7; Matthew 7:7,8; 21:22; Luke 5:16; 18:11-14; Romans 12:3; Hebrews 4:16.

KEY PASSAGE

"Pray continually."

1 Thessalonians 5:17

AIMS OF THE SESSION

During this session your learners will:
1. Discuss why, where, when and with what attitude to pray.
2. Describe ways each element of prayer may be applied to their daily life.
3. Select one thing to pray for.

Young people often avoid prayer because they have found lengthy prayer times boring. Sometimes they are not sure about the "right" time and place for prayer. They may think that Christians can pray only in a church building. They may think you have to spend an hour in prayer, with a lot of complicated requests for missionaries they have never met. Or they don't think God would be interested in what is happening in the life of a junior higher. In addition to these misconceptions, they may find it hard to concentrate. Their minds wander, and it seems like more trouble than it's worth.

This session is designed to provide some antidotes to these problems. It will demonstrate that Christians can pray anytime, anywhere. It will encourage them to believe that God wants to hear about the things that matter to them. It will suggest short frequent prayer times and simple prayers as a way of alleviating boredom and a wandering mind.

Your learners will discover answers to the following questions: 1. Why should we pray? 2. Where can we pray? 3. When should we pray? 4. What is a proper attitude in prayer?

Why should we pray?

The reasons that are covered in the session begin with 1 John 1:9. We pray in order to confess our sins and receive His forgiveness. This course has touched on confession and forgiveness in earlier sessions. When Christians sin they need God's forgiveness and cleansing. Then the burden of the sin is lifted and the person can continue to enjoy God's fellowship and keep on serving Him.

Another reason for prayer is, "Ask and it will be given to you; seek and you will find; knock and the door will be opened to you. For everyone who asks receives; he who seeks finds; and to him who knocks, the door will be opened" (Matt. 7:7,8). In this Scripture, the Lord Jesus issues a generous invitation to pray. We pray in order to ask Him for the things we need. Remind learners that our heavenly Father loves us and wants to meet our needs.

Seeking wisdom is another reason to pray (see Jas. 1:5). Share with students that God wants them to have the benefit of His wisdom. He is happy to give them the wisdom they need for living day by day and for making decisions both large and small. Much of this wisdom is found in His Word, the Bible. He will help young people understand and apply the Scriptures, and thus find His Wisdom, if they make the effort to read and study.

Finally, Christians should pray for one another's needs (see Eph. 6:18). This is an important reason for prayer. Christian teens need to uphold one another in prayer for spiritual growth, ability to resist temptation, and standing firm for the Lord.

You may have a learner who asks, "Why should I pray if God already knows what I'm

NOTES

praying for?" This question overlooks the point that prayer is part of a Christian's relationship with a loving heavenly Father. Even though God knows all about the things we need, He wants us to have the experience of asking Him for them and then seeing Him supply them. Prayer is not so much for God's benefit (informing Him of something) as it is for ours (building our relationship with Him). So we pray, even though we know that God already knows all about it, because it is good for us and for our Christian growth.

Where can we pray?

The point of this part of the session is to show learners that they can pray anywhere. Young people often don't realize this; they somehow pick up the idea that they may pray only in church. This session should liberate them to pray wherever they are.

Peter prayed in Dorcas's room and she was raised from the dead (see Acts 9:39,40). Christians can pray in any room of their home.

The Pharisee and the tax collector prayed in the Temple (see Luke 18:10). The Temple was the building where group worship activities took place. It corresponds to the church building today. Christians may pray in church.

"Jesus often withdrew to lonely places and prayed" (Luke 5:16). Your learners can pray in any place where they can be alone. This aloneness will allow them to concentrate on their conversation with God, and will help reduce interruptions from other people.

Another place where Jesus prayed was at the grave of Lazarus (see John 11:38,41). Prayer will help your learners through all the tragedies and sorrows of life. They can be assured that their Lord understands their sorrow and stands beside them as they go through it.

When can we pray?

David prayed when he was having a problem. "Hear my prayer, O Lord; listen to my cry for mercy. In the day of my trouble I will call to you, for you will answer me" (Ps. 86:6,7). Your learners may call upon the Lord in prayer anytime they have problems and troubles. Nothing is too big or too small for God to listen to and help them with.

Another time to pray is before eating, as exemplified in Jesus' life (see Luke 9:16). It is good to remember the Lord when we eat the food He has provided for us. And it is good to thank Him for other gifts and blessings as well. Suggest to your students that they take time to pray in gratitude when they enjoy His gifts.

The Hebrews developed a custom of praying three times a day, a habit that Daniel pursued even when it nearly cost him his life (see Dan. 6:10). Remind your learners that prayer is for any time of day. It is especially good to begin the day with prayer in order to get started in the right frame of mind (see Ps. 5:3). When young people start the day by laying their needs before God, they can live in quiet confidence that He is caring for them.

Jesus spent a whole night in prayer just before selecting His apostles (see Luke 6:12,13). This provides two hints of when Christians may pray: at night, and before making an important decision. The time of day makes no difference to God; He can hear us anytime. But sometimes it is good to pray at night when the distractions of the day are over.

Prayer before making decisions is also important. Young people need the wisdom God offers and the guidance that He will give if they ask for it. Life can throw many difficult situations in the path of a young person, but prayer will put them in touch with the God who can help them make the right choices.

The final Scripture reference regarding when to pray sums it all up; "Pray continually" (1 Thess. 5:17). Christians can pray any time. There is no time that is an inappropriate or wrong time to pray. God welcomes and urges continual prayer.

What is a proper attitude in prayer?

The attitude or state of mind with which a young person approaches prayer is important. The Scriptures your young people will examine suggest several ingredients that go into a right attitude. Jesus said, "If you believe, you will receive whatever you ask for in prayer" (Matt. 21:22). We need to come to prayer with an attitude of belief. We believe in God—that

He is who He says He is, and that He will do what He has promised. And we come with belief in our request. When we are convinced that we are praying for something that is according to God's will, we can have confidence that He will hear and answer. "This is the assurance we have in approaching God: that if we ask anything according to his will, he hears us. And if we know that he hears us—whatever we ask—we know that we have what we asked of him" (1 John 5:14,15).

Young people can always pray with belief and trust in God and His nature. And often they will be able to pray with the confidence that what they are asking is according to His will. For example, if they confess their sins, they know that it is God's will to forgive and cleanse them (see 1 John 1:9).

But there will be times when students have requests about which they have not been able to ascertain God's will. They may still pray with trust and confidence in God—but they will realize that if the time is not right, God may say, "Wait." And if their request is not the best thing for them, or if it does not fit in with God's sovereign plans, He will say, "No." These are the times when students need to remember the scriptural injunction against anxiety (see Phil. 4:6). Some call this the eleventh commandment: "Thou shalt not sweat." God doesn't want young people worrying and fretting about things. Adolescence is a time when many changes take place in a person's life, and many decisions about the future must be made. It can be a time of uncertainty and anxiety if young people do not learn early to obey Philippians 4:6 and put their trust in God.

Another important thing to notice about Philippians 4:6 is that it says *in everything*. Here is the assurance that God wants to hear the things that are of concern to a young person. He wants His people to pray about everything that is on their minds.

Another important ingredient for a proper attitude in prayer is humility. Jesus told a parable about a Pharisee and a tax collector praying in the Temple. The Pharisee said, "God, I thank you that I am not like all other men—robbers, evildoers, adulterers— or even like this tax collector. I fast twice a week and give a tenth of all I get" (Luke 18:11,12). But the tax

collector prayed, "God, have mercy on me, a sinner" (v.13). Jesus commented, "I tell you that this man, rather than the other, went home justified before God. For everyone who exalts himself will be humbled, and he who humbles himself will be exalted" (v.14). Young people may need some help understanding the meaning of humility. They may incorrectly assume that it means an "I'm-no-good" or a "Step on me. I'm a doormat" attitude. A better grasp of its meaning may be found in Romans 12:3: "Do not think of yourself more highly than you ought." The Pharisee in Jesus' parable was thinking of himself more highly than he ought; he thought he was better than most people, and so he was proud. Jesus' parable warns today's Christians not to get the idea, "I'm one of God's favorite people, and He has to give me exactly what I ask for."

The tax collector, on the other hand, realized that he was a sinner needing God's mercy. Young people need to learn that every human being is a sinner needing God's mercy. No one is God's favorite; the Lord has no "teacher's pets." But He loves and values all of us, as shown by the fact that His Son, Jesus Christ, died in order to provide salvation for us. Thus young people can be confident of God's mercy and His willingness to hear their prayers.

This sort of confidence is mentioned in Hebrews 4:16: "Let us then approach the throne of grace with confidence, so that we may receive mercy and find grace to help us in our time of need." Your learners need to balance humility and confidence. Humility, because, as suggested, all people are sinful and may approach God only because of His mercy and grace; confidence, because God does offer that mercy and grace and invites each believer to come to Him in prayer, trusting Him for the right answers.

NOTES

SESSION PLAN

BEFORE CLASS BEGINS: Photocopy the "Prayer Chart" from the "Clip Art and Other Goodies" section. See page 90 for details.

Attention Grabber

ATTENTION GRABBER (8-10 minutes)

Step 1 (2-3 minutes): Instruct your students, **On the blank side of your Treasure Seeker worksheet, write the initials of the person you most enjoy talking with. Then list as many reasons as you can why talking with that person is so enjoyable.**

Step 2 (2-3 minutes): When everyone has completed the assignment, ask them why they enjoy talking with the person they selected. On a chalkboard or a sheet of newsprint, list at least five answers.

Some of the answers might include, "It's fun to talk to this person," "He has interesting things to say," "She listens," "She likes me," "We like the same things." Comment that it is pleasant to communicate with someone who likes us and who can enjoy the same things we enjoy. It feels good when someone listens to us and when we have a good time together.

Say something like, **We enjoy talking to people. And we can also enjoy talking to God. That's what prayer is. Let's look at the reasons for talking to a person, and see which of them apply to talking to God.**

Step 3 (2-3 minutes): Read through the list aloud and have students tell you which items apply to talking to God. Put a star beside these. Then say, **Today we are going to learn about talking to God in prayer.**

Bible Exploration

EXPLORATION (20-35 minutes)

Step 1 (5-10 minutes): Have students form groups of three or four for this part of the assignment. Each group will work on one or more of the first three questions in the "An Odyssey on Prayer" section of the Treasure Seeker student worksheet. Assign each group one question to complete (more than one if you don't have three groups. If you have four or more groups, several groups can work on each question.) If a group finishes early, they may work on a second or third question.

Step 2 (5-10 minutes): When all of the groups have completed their assignments, regain the attention of the class by saying,

Let's go over the answers one by one. In the first question, what reason does 1 John 1:9

give for prayer? List their answers on the chalkboard. Then provide any further guidance that may be needed, drawing from the INSIGHTS FOR THE LEADER and from the ideas that follow.

The first question is **Why should we pray?** Students should discover that some of the reasons for prayer include these: we pray to confess sins and receive forgiveness, to present our requests to God, to seek wisdom, and to intercede for other Christians. Be sure to point out that your students can pray about anything. There is nothing they cannot talk to God about. Ask for volunteers to suggest some things that young people today might want to pray about. These might include their relationships with family and friends; school; sharing Christ; their personal needs, whether material, emotional, or spiritual; the ministry of their church to people outside its walls; missionaries, and so on.

The second question is, **Where can we pray?** They will find that Bible people prayed in a person's room, in the Temple (analogous to a church building), in lonely places, and beside a grave. A Christian can pray anywhere he or she happens to be.

Ask for volunteers to suggest places where Christian young people today can pray. These might include at home, while riding in a car or on a bike, at school, while spending time with friends, while doing homework, and so on.

Other questions to ask include the following: **Where have you found it easy to pray? What is an unusual place where you have prayed? Why do some people find it helpful to select a specific place where they pray?**

The third question is, **When can we pray?** Students will find that Bible people prayed when in trouble, before a meal, three times a day, in the morning, all night, before making important decisions. The Bible says to pray continually. A Christian can pray at any time, for God is always listening.

Ask for volunteers to suggest times when a Christian young person can pray. Their ideas at first might not go beyond the responses to the Scripture search, so encourage them to think of specific situations in which young people might want to

pray, such as the following: while studying for a test, before taking the test, before sharing Christ with a friend, before an important discussion with parents about new privileges and responsibilities, and so on.

Step 3 (3-5 minutes): When the discussion is concluded, say, **Now, I want you to work again in the same small groups to complete the next part of this assignment. Everyone will respond to the fourth question in the "An Odyssey on Prayer" section of the Treasure Seeker.**

Step 4 (5-10 minutes): When students have completed the assignment, have them report their findings as you list them on chalkboard or newsprint. Then provide any further guidance that may be needed, drawing from the INSIGHTS FOR THE LEADER and from the ideas that follow.

Students are discovering proper attitudes in prayer. These begin with **belief**—believing in God and believing that your request is according to His will. Ask for volunteers to suggest some prayers that young people might be able to pray according to God's will. Answers might include praying for the salvation of others, praying that God will make them more Christlike, praying for God's power in witnessing.

Another attitude needed in prayer is one of **trusting God** rather than being anxious. Ask for volunteers to suggest how praying about problems will help young people stop worrying about those situations. Guide them to see that prayer helps us focus our minds on God, so that we remember His greatness and His desire to help us. As we focus on His power rather than on the problem, we can relax and trust Him to take care of it.

Humility is also needed in prayer. Ask for volunteers to share their ideas on what humility is. Then guide them to see that it is not thinking more of yourself than you should (see INSIGHTS FOR THE LEADER for more details).

Finally, God urges His children to approach Him **confidently**. Ask for volunteers to describe the difference between approaching God without confidence and with confidence. (A person without confidence may not be sure that God exists, or that He hears prayers, or that He cares about the person

NOTES

praying. A person with confidence in God knows that He exists, that He hears prayer, that He cares, and that He will answer the prayer in the best possible way.)

If it seems appropriate, you may wish to deal briefly with the following questions which often trouble young people:

What do you do when you don't feel like praying? Probably the simplest way to deal with this feeling is to be honest and say, "Lord, I don't feel like praying." That, in itself, is a prayer. And it often breaks the ice and helps a person feel more in the mood for talking to God.

How can you keep your mind on prayer? One thing that helps is praying short prayers throughout the day. It's easier to keep your mind on five different one-topic prayers scattered throughout the day than on one long prayer covering five topics.

Another thing that will help young people keep their minds on prayer is to pray about things that are important and interesting to them. This will automatically make them more apt to pay attention to what they are praying.

What should I pray about? Here, too, suggest to young people that they pray about anything and everything that is of concern to them. Friends, family, pets, problems in school, a desire to make the soccer team—all of these are appropriate for prayer. Then, as young people's horizons expand, they might pray about the ministry of their local church, for the salvation of the lost, and other such matters.

Conclusion and Decision

CONCLUSION (8-10 minutes)

Materials needed: The Prayer Chart from the "Clip Art and Other Goodies" section at the end of this book.

Say something like this: **Remember that God is our loving heavenly Father. He is interested in every aspect of our lives, our needs, desires, feelings, circumstances. There is nothing that we cannot talk to Him about. We never have to wait to pray. We can and should be ready to pray any time, anywhere. You don't have to kneel or close your eyes. You can talk to God while riding your bicycle or walking down the street. We've learned a lot about talking to God today. Have you been considering some new ideas about how to improve this relationship in your life? Perhaps you have not thought about praying in a certain situation or place before, or talking to God about something that has been troubling you.**

Take a look at the Prayer Chart that I am handing out. If you regularly use this chart as you pray, it will help you develop a good habit of effective prayer. Right now I want you to write today's date in the "Date" column. Then, working individually, write one thing you want to thank God for in the "Praises" column, and one thing you want to ask Him for in the "Requests" column. Perhaps you could ask Him to help a friend in need of salvation or a family member who is ill. Leave the "Answers" column blank until God answers your request. When He does, jot down the date.

Invite learners to share what they have written with you privately so that you can encourage them and pray for them during the week.

Close in prayer. As students leave, again encourage them to save and use their Prayer Charts. Distribute the Fun Page take-home paper.

An Odyssey on Prayer

1. WHY? These verses tell a few of the reasons for prayer. What are they?

1 John 1:9 _____

Matthew 7:7,8 _____

James 1:5 _____

Ephesians 6:18 _____

3. WHEN? When did the people mentioned in the following verses pray? What does this tell you about when you can pray?

Psalm 86:6,7 _____

Luke 9:16 _____

Daniel 6:10 _____

Psalm 5:3 _____

Luke 6:12,13 _____

When does 1 Thessalonians 5:17 say to pray? _____

2. WHERE? Where did the people mentioned in the following verses pray? What does this tell you about where you can pray?

Acts 9:39,40 _____

Luke 18:10 _____

Luke 5:16 _____

John 11:38,41 _____

4. WITH WHAT ATTITUDE? What do the following verses tell you about the kinds of attitudes you should have when praying?

Mattthew 21:22 _____

Phillippians 4:6 _____

Luke 18:10-14 _____

Hebrews 4:16 _____

HIT OR MISS!

 "Ask and it will be given to you."
Matthew 7:7

 "If any of you lacks wisdom, he should ask God."
James 1:5

 "And pray in the Spirit on all occasions."
Ephesians 6:18

"In the day of my trouble I will call to you, for you will answer me."
Psalm 86:7

"But Jesus often withdrew to lonely places and prayed."
Luke 5:16

"If you believe, you will receive whatever you ask for in prayer."
Matthew 21:22

"Pray continually."
1 Thessalonians 5:17

Here's a fun test of skills that will teach you an important lesson about prayer.

Rules:

Put the point of your pen or pencil on the "Praying Hands" at the bottom of the game. With your eyes closed, try to draw a line from the hands to any of the stars. Now open your eyes. If you hit the star, award yourself ten points. If you missed or overshot the star, subtract two points from your score. The game is over when you have hit all seven stars.

 Praying Hands

A good lesson about prayer: Unlike this game we call **"HIT OR MISS,"** *real* prayer is not a hit or miss affair—God does not listen to a few of your prayers and ignore others. God *always* hears you when you talk with Him. First John 5:14,15 tells us, "This is the confidence we have in approaching God: that if we ask anything according to his will, he hears us. And if we know that he hears us—whatever we ask— we know that we have what we asked of him." So if you are seeking to be in the center of God's will, He will hear you and He will make sure the proper answer is delivered to you.

DAILY NUGGETS

Day 1   Read Romans 8:26,27. Who can you count on to help you when you are not sure how to pray?

Day 2   1 John 3:21,22; 5:14,15. Here are some requirements for answered prayer: obey God, do what pleases Him, and pray according to what?

Day 3   Ephesians 1:17. What prayer request is found in this passage? Is there someone for whom you could pray this request?

Day 4   Ephesians 1:18,19. What prayer requests are found in this passage? How do you need God's power in your life today?

Day 5   Philippians 1:9-11. List people (including yourself) for whom you can pray the prayer.

Day 6   1 Thessalonians 5:16-18. What connection can you see between rejoicing (being joyful), prayer, and giving thanks?

If you can't remember this one, you're not trying.

"Pray continually."
1 Thessalonians 5:17

THEME: God likes to hear from us.

BIBLE STUDY OUTLINE

Read Luke 11:5-13 to your students. Discuss these points as time allows:

- Jesus uses humor in this parable. Waking up at midnight to a moocher at your door was just as big a headache back then as it is now.
- But in verse 8, persistence pays off. Jesus is teaching us that it pays to be persistent in prayer; not just persistent in one particular prayer, but persistently praying as a habit. In this instance, God seems to love moochers!
- Jesus told this story to show us what God is NOT like. He is not like the sleepy neighbor who has to be hassled over and over again before responding to our needs. He wants to hear our requests.
- In verses 9 and 10, Jesus makes an important promise: anyone who asks and seeks will find. Anyone who knocks, even at midnight, will discover that the door swings open. This is the secret to successful living: persistently stick close to God, seeking Him for all things.
- Evil people know how to give good gifts (see verses 11-13). How much more a loving God knows how to give! Jesus claims He gives us the greatest gift of all: the Holy Spirit.

OBJECT LESSON: COINS

Hand out quarters, one per student. Ask each student to examine the coin in his or her hand.

Hold up a coin for all to see. Say something like, **If you turn over your coin, you will notice that there is another side to this coin—and there is another side to prayer: often, when we ask God for something, He expects us to become involved in answering that prayer. For example, if you pray that God will lead a friend to salvation, God may expect you to invite your friend to our Bible study. Or if you pray that the homeless in our town will be helped, He might ask you to contribute time or money.**

Jesus said that faith can move mountains. But if you pray for a mountain to be moved, don't be surprised if God gives you a shovel and the strength to dig!

Allow students to keep the coins as a memento of the lesson.

DISCUSSION QUESTIONS

1. **What does the word "persistence" mean?**
2. **What difference do you see between the type of persistence a Christian is supposed to have in prayer, and the persistence a little child displays when he or she whines and nags for a toy?**
3. **If our youth group had an attitude of being persistently in prayer, in what ways do you think our group would be different?**
4. **What are five things a Christian your age should be praying about every day?**
5. **Jesus said that anyone who seeks, finds. Why do you suppose some people never seem to find their way in life?**
6. **Why do you suppose Jesus is excited about God giving us the Holy Spirit? Who is the Holy Spirit and what are some of the things He does for us?**

THE COMPLETE JUNIOR HIGH
BIBLE STUDY RESOURCE
BOOK #1

Here are a few games that require persistence.

"SHOE TOSS"

Everybody removes his or her shoes and tosses them into one big pile in the center of the floor. After putting on blindfolds, players are led to the pile, where they are to attempt to identify and put on their own shoes. As you observe the action, you might tell players what color shoes they are holding or other helpful hints. For fun, make participants wear the shoes they have chosen for the rest of the meeting.

"LUNG DESTROYER"

Mark a line on the floor and assemble two teams as illustrated:

Place several dozen cotton balls on the line. At a signal, players are to blow as many of the cotton balls into the opponents' side as possible. Players must walk on their knees. No hands allowed.

After a reasonable time (just before players turn blue) bring the game to a halt. The team with the fewest cotton balls on its side wins.

VARIATION:

Allow the two teams to cheer as two designated representatives attempt to blow the cotton balls toward each other across a short line while blindfolded.

"SLOW MOTION RELAY"

This is a typical relay race, with one catch. As players run the course, they must hold on to their legs as shown. Anyone who lets go while racing must start over. Incidentally, this is a *great way to wear out your kids.*

The Church

WHAT THE SESSION IS ABOUT

The Church is God's family. Family members enjoy benefits and have responsibilities.

SCRIPTURE STUDIED

Galatians 6:2,5,10; Ephesians 5:1,2; 1 Thessalonians 5:11.

KEY PASSAGE

"Therefore, as we have opportunity, let us do good to all people, especially to those who belong to the family of believers."
                                    Galatians 6:10

AIMS OF THE SESSION

During this session your learners will:
1. Define what is meant by the Church and list responsibilities of the Church to believers and of believers to the Church.
2. Name at least one example of how a junior higher could fulfill each responsibility.
3. Indicate a specific way in which they personally could contribute to the Church this week.

INSIGHTS FOR THE LEADER

This session focuses on the Church as the family of believers—as *people*—and on the responsibilities believers have toward their fellow family members. You and your students will study six responsibilities from six Bible passages. This INSIGHTS FOR THE LEADER will provide you with important ideas to use during class time.

1. Imitate God

"Be imitators of God, therefore, as dearly loved children" (Eph. 5:1). Young children love to imitate their parents. God's children should imitate their heavenly Father. We know what God is like because His Son Jesus is an exact representation of His nature (see Heb. 1:3). To imitate God, then, is to be like Christ. We are like Christ when we are caring, fair, giving, honest, honorable, and so forth. A junior high student might have a hard time grasping the concept of imitating God, but he or she can understand the ideas of caring, being fair, etc. (Session 9 looks at imitating Christ in more detail.)

2. A Life of Love

"And live a life of love, just as Christ loved us and gave himself up for us as a fragrant offering and sacrifice to God" (Eph. 5:2).

Christ is the great example of love. He gave Himself up to die on the cross for us. He set aside His divine privileges in order to live on earth among the human race for some 30 years. He came to meet our needs, not to have us meet His needs. This is the kind of love Christians should imitate, the kind of love that only God's power within can produce. As Christians let the Spirit control them, and as they make a conscious effort to determine and to do the loving thing in each situation, they will find themselves growing more and more Christlike.

3. Carry Burdens

One way to show love to other Christians is to "**carry each other's burdens**" (Gal. 6:2). The word used in this verse for "burden" means "something heavy," and may refer to a fault, a weakness, a pressure, a tension, an ignorance, or a grief. These are the kinds of burdens which one Christian can help another bear.

If one person has a fault, another can point it out in a loving manner and help with suggestions for ways to overcome it. If one is weak, another may spend time with him or her, sharing Scripture and other helpful material that will strengthen the weakness.

If a Christian is undergoing some pressure or tension, another can stand alongside and help that one. Maybe one student is having an especially difficult time in a particular class. A friend might take time to go over the homework and the study materials with that person,

NOTES

helping him or her understand the concepts that are difficult.

If someone is ignorant, particularly regarding scriptural truth about God and Jesus and salvation or Christian growth, another Christian can help with that burden by teaching and discipling that person.

When a person is undergoing grief, perhaps because of the illness or death of a loved one, another Christian can help bear the burden just by being there. It is a great help to the suffering person to have someone care, show an interest, stand with him or her. Sometimes the grieving person needs to talk about the situation to a willing listener; sometimes silent companionship is all that is needed. A believer who is helping to bear another's burden of grief will learn when to listen, when to speak, and when to let silence prevail.

4. Bear Own Load

There is another kind of burden that each person must carry alone: **"For each one should carry his own load"** (Gal. 6:5). In this case the word for load or burden means "a load to be borne." J.B. Phillips' *New Testament in Modern English* paraphrases it this way: "For every man must 'shoulder his own pack.'" This means taking care of one's own responsibilities.

Each person must "shoulder his own pack" in terms of being responsible for his or her relationship with the Lord. No one is a Christian because his parents know Christ; no one is excused from making a choice about commitment just because her family background omitted any mention of Him.

Each Christian is responsible for maintaining his or her spiritual life through Bible study and prayer, church attendance and fellowship. Each one has responsibilities within the family of God, such as giving money to support the church, participating in activities, and helping with the work needed to accomplish them. For example, Christians should reach out to be friendly to others instead of waiting for others to be friendly first. Other examples might be helping the janitor clean up after an activity, or ushering, or singing in a choir. There are many ways to carry one's share of responsibility in a local fellowship.

5. Do Good

Another responsibility of Christians is to **"do good to all people, especially to those who belong to the family of believers"** (Gal. 6:10). Christian love is not exclusive; believers are to do good to all people. They can be friendly to the friendless at school; mow a lawn or run an errand for a neighbor; share Christ's love with those who have not met Him. They can visit elderly or lonely people; they can sponsor an orphan or other needy child; they can help out at Vacation Bible School or other children's events. And they are to be especially aware of needs within the family of God, for these people are brothers and sisters in Christ.

6. Encourage

Finally, Christians are to **"encourage one another and build each other up"** (1 Thess. 5:11). They are to help each other grow in the Lord. When one is discouraged, another should offer encouragement. When one is confused about a passage of Scripture, another should try to help figure it out. When one is uncertain about a personal decision, another should pray with him or her, seeking God's direction. Christians should be a team, working together to develop each other's faith and ability to live for God.

SESSION PLAN

Attention Grabber

ATTENTION GRABBER (3-5 minutes)

When students arrive, say **I want you to write down what you feel is the most important contribution you make to your family. Perhaps you'll feel it's a certain chore or responsibility. Maybe you think it's the love and affection you show family members. Whatever it is, write it down.**

Let students work for a minute. Then say, **Now write down what you feel is the best benefit you receive from your family.**

When all have finished writing, ask volunteers to share their thoughts. Make a transition to the EXPLORATION by pointing out that all true Christians are members of another family: God's family.

Say, **The Church—the family of all Christians around the world—is God's family** here on earth. **As a member of God's Church, you have important responsibilities to other family members. And there are wonderful benefits you can receive from the other family members. Today we are going to look at a few of these responsibilities and benefits.**

CREATIVE OPTION (5-7 minutes)

When everyone has arrived, tell them **Draw a quick sketch of the Church.**

Most or all of your students will probably draw a church building. Point out that the real church is constructed not of wood or bricks, but of people. Then proceed with the original Attention Grabber.

Bible Exploration

EXPLORATION (30-40 minutes)

Step 1 (10-12 minutes): Quickly sketch the outline of a church building on your chalkboard or on a large sheet of butcher paper, along with the heading, "What's In It For You?," as shown in the illustration.

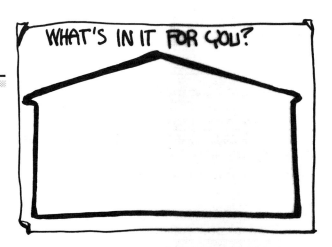

WHAT'S IN IT FOR YOU?

NOTES

Say, **This rough sketch represents the church building, which is where the Church—God's family—comes together for fellowship and other purposes. But what's in it for you? What are some of the reasons why you come together here in the church building?**

As students respond, write their answers in the sketch of the building. Encourage learners to give the genuine reasons why they come; to meet with friends, to play sports at "games night" and so on. Be sure to cover the ideas of worship, community prayer, fellowship, Bible study, and so on.

When finished, lead a short discussion pointing out how each of the suggestions are really *benefits* for your students to enjoy. Then say, **These are "what's in it for you": friendship, enjoyment, fun, learning about God, learning about life, and help from caring people when you have needs or problems. These are some of the benefits of being in God's family.**

Step 2 (10-12 minutes): List these verses in a column on your board or paper:

Ephesians 5:1
Galatians 6:2
Galatians 6:5
Ephesians 5:2
Galatians 6:10
1 Thessalonians 5:11

Then say, **Most of us have certain ideas about what we want out of the Church. As with most areas of life, we have to accept responsibilities in order to have privileges. Everyone who wants to benefit from the Church also needs to contribute in some way. We're going to take a look at some of the ways we can contribute.**

Have a volunteer read the first verse aloud. Ask the class what responsibility the verse describes. (Ephesians 5:1 says to imitate God.) Write down the correct response next to the verse. Do this for each passage, being sure that learners have a clear understanding of each response.

Step 3 (10-15 minutes): Tell your class, **Now find the "How Can We Do It?" section on the Treasure Seeker student worksheet. Let's think of some practical ways people your age could meet some of the responsibilities listed.**

Lead a discussion of the practical ways of meeting responsibilities. Ask questions like these: **How can we bear one another's burdens? What can we do to build others up? What would our church be like if no one did these things?** Use ideas from INSIGHTS FOR THE LEADER to supplement students' contributions.

Conclusion and Decision

CONCLUSION (3-5 minutes)

Write on the chalkboard or overhead:

"This week I will benefit from God's family by . . ."

"This week I will help God's family by . . ."

Tell learners, **Think for a moment of the benefits and responsibilities we have discussed today. Then finish each sentence by writing one thing you will do.**

Allow students time to work. Close in prayer. As students leave, distribute the Fun Page take-home paper.

How Can We Do It?

	At Home	At Church
Bear own burden (Carry our own weight)		
Bear another's burden (Help with problem)		
Do good to others		
Walk in love (Communicate a loving attitude)		
Imitate God		
Encourage each other		

A MAZE ZINGER!

OK, maze fans. Put your pencil on the starting block and draw your way to the church. The paths cross over and under each other.

When you have finished (or when you give up):

Did you find it impossible to blaze a trail to the church? If so, you blew it. You were trying to draw a line to the church *building*. The real church is not a building. The real church is people: Christians! See that little group of people in the corner of the maze? They are the church. We sure fooled you, eh? A-MAZE-ING!

DAILY NUGGETS

Day 1 Read Ephesians 4:25. This verse says we are all members of what? What responsibility do we have toward fellow members?

Day 2 Ephesians 4:31,32. Do you need to get rid of some bitterness, anger, etc.? Is there someone you need to work things out with?

Day 3 Colossians 3:12-17. What one thing in this Scripture passage do you most need to work on? What will you do about it today?

Day 4 1 Thessalonians 5:11. Name someone who encouraged you when you were down. Is there someone who could use your help now?

Day 5 James 2:2-9. Here's a practical way to show responsibility to other members of the church: treat them all alike, with fairness and justice.

Day 6 James 2:15,16. Is there something you can do this week to help meet the needs of another believer?

"Therefore, as we have opportunity, let us do good to all people, especially to those who belong to the family of believers."
Galatians 6:10

THE COMPLETE JUNIOR HIGH BIBLE STUDY RESOURCE BOOK #1
© 1987 GL/LIGHT FORCE, VENTURA, CA 93006

THEME: The youth group members are important parts of God's church body.

BIBLE STUDY OUTLINE

Study 1 Corinthians 12:12-18 with your students. Make these remarks as time permits:

- It takes all body parts working together for a person to be whole and complete. A person who is blind, has a missing leg or other impairment is called *handicapped,* an unpopular label.
- This youth group is also a body, a body of people who love the Lord. It takes all of us working together to be complete and strong. It takes all pieces in a puzzle to complete the picture. All bricks must be in place before a wall is sturdy.
- God has given each person in this group an important purpose and set of abilities. United, we can serve the Lord and remain strong in Him. Separated, we miss so very much.
- This is why attendance at these meetings—the special events and fun trips as well as the Bible studies—is so important. When you are gone, not only are you missing out, but so are we.
- This is also why it is important to come prepared—willing and able to make some contribution. Your contribution could be anything from helping set up chairs or bringing a friend, to listening to a pal's problems after the meeting.
- And don't forget: it is God who has made you what you are. You needn't worry about what sort of contributions you can make or how you fit in. If you are willing to do so, God will work things out. You just be here.

OBJECT LESSON:
THE BODY THAT WASN'T THERE

For this lesson you need a poster of a face, large enough for the entire group to see, and scissors.

Say something like, **Pretend that this picture represents the body of believers in this room. Each feature on this face represents some important and necessary function or ability that our group has. For example, the eyes represent *insight,* the special talent some of you have to quickly grasp spiritual truths in the Bible.**

The mouth could stand for those who have the ability to help friends with *words of kindness or wisdom*—not everyone in this group has that valuable skill.

The ears might represent the talent for *listening and showing sympathy* to people who come for help.

And couldn't the nose represent *sensitivity* to situations or problems that just aren't right—just as a nose can smell trouble?

This would be a pretty boring group if we were all noses! Actually, each of us has our own special purpose as a part of this Christian group. Together, we form a complete "face." So everyone here is an important part of the group. We each have a purpose and usefulness.

Now, as you talk about the problem of group members who don't show up or contribute to the welfare of the group, use the scissors to cut out various parts of the face. Throw the parts on the floor as you snip them out.

DISCUSSION QUESTIONS

1. Have you ever smashed your thumb with a hammer or done some other extremely painful thing? If so, how did it affect your ability to work and play and do the things you ordinarily do?
2. When a Christian is hurting or getting into wrong things, do you think that affects the whole group? In what ways?
3. Name the things a human body needs to stay alive and healthy. You've said, among other things, that a body needs food. What sort of "food" does our group need to stay healthy? What do the other things you mentioned teach us?
4. How can a person begin to learn what he or she is best at in serving the Lord in this group?
5. What would you tell a person who feels he or she has nothing of value to contribute?
6. What are some things we could be doing that would make us a better group?

The body is not all thumbs, is it? Find out with these challengers.

"RUNNING WATER"

Form two teams. Line students on their backs, feet up as shown. Teams are to pass various objects (listed below) from one end to the other. Any object dropped must be started over. First team to pass all objects wins.

Here are some suggestions for the objects:

Ball (volleyball, soccer or basketball)
Pillow or sofa cushion
Beanbag
Thick store catalogue
Watermelon
Well-filled water balloon

Finally, when one or both teams appear to be nearly finished, reveal the final object each must pass: a plastic pail filled to the brim with water.

"AN OBJECT—TIONABLE RELAY"

A relay race for two or more teams. Each team assembles into couples. Each couple must pick up an object (could be some of those mentioned above) and transport it the length of the race track or obstacle course. They cannot touch the object with their hands or feet; they can pick up and transport the object only with head, shoulders, or middle part of the body. If time permits, you might want the teams to cycle through several different objects.

VARIATION: Couples can only touch and transport the object with their feet. Their feet may not touch the ground at any time. This requires a lot of time and effort, so make the race course small.

"TABLE BASKETBALL"

This is a good carnival-style game. Nail Styrofoam or paper cups to plywood. Use a marker to write point values on the cups, the higher points in the middle "bulls eye" cups. Make a "wobble ball" by putting a penny into an under-inflated balloon. Contestants stand back a few feet and try to score points by tossing the balloon into the cups.

Incidentally, the balloon wobble ball is great for other ball games such as broom hockey or golf.

Imitators of Him

INSIGHTS FOR THE LEADER

WHAT THE SESSION IS ABOUT

Some of the characteristics of Christ that a young believer can imitate.

SCRIPTURE STUDIED

Matthew 11:29; Mark 6:34; Luke 2:51, 23:34; John 13:34; 14:31; 15:10; Galatians 5:22,23; 1 Timothy 1:16.

KEY PASSAGE

"Be imitators of God, therefore, as dearly loved children."

Ephesians 5:1

AIMS OF THE SESSION

During this session your learners will:

1. Identify Christ as the Christian's model in life.
2. List characteristics of a Christlike life.
3. Select ways to make their life-style more like Christ's.

This session focuses on the need for believers to model or imitate Christ in order to influence others for Him. After considering the importance of living up to one's profession, students will examine selected characteristics of Christ that His followers, with the help of the Holy Spirit, can imitate in their own lives.

Love

Jesus said, "As I have loved you, so you must love one another" (John 13:34). His love is shown by the fact that He laid down His life for us (see 1 John 3:16). Love means wanting the best for the loved person and doing whatever is necessary to accomplish that best. Loving as Christ loves is not a matter of emotions and feelings. Love is a decision to give and to serve another.

Love sometimes requires sacrifices by the loving person in order to accomplish what is needed for the loved one. Jesus sacrificed for us throughout the Incarnation. He left the glories of heaven in order to become a man; He lived and ministered on earth; and then He suffered the Crucifixion for our sake. While your young people are not likely to have occasion to die for someone else, they can "lay down their lives" in imitation of Christ by setting aside their self-centered desires in order to minister to the needs of others. They can seek out what is best for others and make sacrifices in order to accomplish that best.

Compassion

Scripture says that when He "saw a large crowd, he had compassion on them" (Mark 6:34). Compassion means sympathy, pity, responsiveness to people. This is a quality teenagers often lack. Their insecurity about their own identify often blocks them from being sensitive to the needs of others. They may ridicule the young person who looks different, who is a little too dumb or a little too smart, who isn't good at sports or doesn't fit in with the activities of the rest of the crowd. They may ignore and exclude those who don't conform to their set ideas of what a friend should be and do. In contrast, Jesus took time with the misfits, the handicapped, the ill. He gave of His energy to be with them and to help them. And through the Holy Spirit, He can enable His followers to show the same compassion for those who don't quite fit in to society's pattern.

Humble and Gentle

He said, "Take my yoke upon you and learn from me, for I am gentle and humble in heart, and you will find rest for your souls" (Matt. 11:29). Jesus' humility, like His love, is demonstrated in His willingness to come to earth as a human being, to live a life of ministry to others, and to die for our sake. Humility does not mean having a low opinion of yourself. It means being willing to put someone

NOTES

else's problems ahead of your own. His gentleness was evident in the way He lived and ministered. He encouraged little children to come to Him (see Matthew 19:14) and He held and blessed them (see Mark 10:16)—signs of gentleness. He went willingly to the cross, without lashing out at those who tormented and executed Him. He assured the thief on the cross that he would be with Him in paradise (see Luke 23:43). He forgave those who crucified Him (see Luke 23:34). All these are evidences of His gentleness and His strength. Many young people confuse gentleness with weakness, missing the skill and power required of those who are gentle.

Young people may imitate Christ's humility and gentleness in the way they treat others. These two qualities are tied in with love and compassion. They all work together to produce a person who is kind to and considerate of others and who is willing to give of self to meet others' needs.

Obedient

Jesus said, "The world must learn that I love the Father and that I do exactly what my Father has commanded me" (John 14:31); and, "If you obey my commands, you will remain in my love, just as I have obeyed my Father's commands and remain in his love" (John 15:10). Because Jesus obeyed the Father in His life on earth, even to the point of dying on the cross, we can enjoy the salvation thus provided. Young people can imitate Christ's obedience by doing what God wants as they live day to day. God's instructions are found in the Bible. As young people read and study the Word, they will find specific instructions about what pleases Him and how He wants them to live. For example, if a young person is tempted to shoplift, he or she will find that God's Word says that stealing is wrong. Obeying God's will then means that the young person will not shoplift, since that is stealing.

As a child, Jesus obeyed His parents. After the incident in which He stayed behind in the Temple at Jerusalem, "He went down to Nazareth with [his parents] and was obedient to them" (Luke 2:51). He obeyed His earthly parents even though He was God. Christian young people can model His obedi-

ence by submitting to their parents. God gives people parents because babies and children and young people need guidance and protection by someone who is older and who knows more about life. Obedience to parents can keep young people from making many serious mistakes. Even if parents don't know the Lord, they can provide guidance about life and protect their children from mistakes and harm that might come to them. Christian parents provide an added benefit in that they can give guidance in knowing God and His Word.

Patience

Paul Speaks of Christ's "unlimited patience" (1 Tim. 1:16). Patience is a calm and kindly response to people who oppose us and treat us harshly. Jesus' patience was displayed most forcefully in the Crucifixion incidents discussed under "humble and gentle." Christian young people can imitate Christ's patience by responding with kindness to people who harass them. When they witness and people reject the gospel harshly, Christians can respond with patience, rather than yielding to the temptation to respond harshly in turn.

Forgiving

Even as He was being crucified, He prayed for those who were killing Him: "Father, forgive them, for they do not know what they are doing" (Luke 23:34). He did not hold their deeds against them. Christian young people benefit from His forgiveness, for when they sin they have only to confess the sin in order to experience forgiveness and cleansing (see 1 John 1:9). God removes our iniquities from us as far as the east is from the west (see Ps. 103:12). Therefore, the young believer should also imitate Christ by forgiving others. Holding grudges and nursing anger against others is unChristlike. If young people find it hard to forgive, they may come to God and ask Him to help them.

These characteristics are just the beginning of learning to be like Christ. Encourage your young people to study God's Word in order to learn about Christ and to invite the Holy Spirit to work in their lives to make them more like the Saviour.

SESSION PLAN

Attention Grabber

ATTENTION GRABBER (5-7 minutes)

Draw a stick figure on the chalkboard or overhead as shown:

Ask students to think of a real or imaginary hero they had when they were younger. When students have made several suggestions, tell them, **Let's build our own hero on this stick figure. You tell me some of the characteristics and outstanding traits of your heroes, and I'll try to draw them on the board.**

As your learners respond, quickly sketch their ideas. For example, if someone says her hero was good, draw a white hat on the stick figure. If the hero was strong, add muscles or a can of spinach. If it was a basketball star, lengthen the legs or put the head in a hoop. Have fun with this and don't worry about the appearance of the drawing. When your drawing is complete, you should have a very strange hero!

Ask students to raise their hand if they ever wished they could be like their personal heroes.

Make a transition to the next part of the session by saying something like this: **We've been talking about heroes and how we sometimes try to become more like them. As Christians, we need to try to become more like Jesus Christ. He is not a "hero" in the same way as Superman or Wonder Woman or other "superheroes." He is far greater than they are, and He is real while they are imaginary. Even if our hero is an older brother or sister, a sports figure, or some other real person, Jesus Christ is far greater than any human being, for He is God. It's fun to have heroes, whether they are imaginary, like Superman, or real, like a football player, but it is even more exciting and worthwhile to have Jesus Christ as our example. Especially since we can cooperate with the Holy Spirit as He works in us to actually make us more like Jesus. We're going to look at what Jesus is like so we'll know what kind of an example we are to follow.**

109

NOTES

Bible Exploration

EXPLORATION (15-30 minutes)

Step 1 (5-6 minutes): Tell students, **On your Treasure Seeker worksheet is a section titled "In His Steps." Work in pairs to look up the Scriptures I assign you and write down what they say about characteristics of Christ. In other words, what is He like? Is He patient or impatient, loving or crabby, kind or stern?** Assign each pair of students two or three Scriptures from the worksheets, duplicating assignments as needed. Let students work. Be available to guide them and to answer questions.

Step 2 (5-6 minutes): Ask for volunteers to report some of their findings. Students should find the characteristics listed below. Draw from the INSIGHTS FOR THE LEADER to amplify student reports if needed.

Jesus is **loving.** He said, "As I have loved you, so you must love one another" (John 13:34).

He is **compassionate.** When He "saw a large crowd, he had compassion on them" (Mark 6:34). (Compassion means sympathy, pity, responsiveness to people.)

He is **humble and gentle.** He said, "Take my yoke upon you and learn from me, for I am gentle and humble in heart, and you will find rest for your souls" (Matt. 11:29).

He is **obedient to God's will.** He said, "The world must learn that I love the Father and that I do exactly what my Father has commanded me" (John 14:31); and, "If you obey my commands, you will remain in my love, just as I have obeyed my Father's commands and remain in his love" (John 15:10).

As a child, Jesus **obeyed His parents.** After the incident in which He stayed behind in the Temple at Jerusalem, "He went down to Nazareth with [his parents] and was obedient to them" (Luke 2:51).

Even the Son of God obeyed the earthly parents that His heavenly Father had given to Him.

Jesus is **patient.** Paul speaks of His "unlimited patience" (1 Tim. 1:16).

He is **forgiving.** Even as He was being crucified, He prayed for those who were killing Him: "Father, forgive them, for they do not know what they are doing" (Luke 23:34).

Step 3 (5-6 minutes): Lead a discussion, using questions like these to get it started: **What kind of person would you rather be around—one with the characteristics of Christ, or one without them? How would you rather be treated? If you were hurting, would you want someone to be compassionate to you? If you were trying to learn a new sport, would you want the people who are good at it to criticize you and be harsh with you, or to be patient while you were learning? How do you feel when you are with a person who is cold or mean or egotistical? How does a loving, humble person affect the people around him or her?** (Remind students that humility does not mean having a low opinion of yourself. It means being realistic about yourself, and being willing to put another person's problems or needs ahead of your own.) **Would a kind, loving person have more friends or fewer friends than an unkind, unloving person? Would a compassionate person be the kind of person you would want to spend time with? If you sprained your ankle playing ball, what kind of person would you want to have around?**

OPTIONAL ALTERNATIVE TO *STEP 3* (10-12 minutes)

Now I want you to select at least one of the characteristics of Jesus and work in pairs to draw a cartoon strip in which you show modern day examples of that characteristic in action. For example, what would happen at your school if someone was patient or loving or forgiving? What problems would occur? How could the person deal with these problems? What would happen in the home if a young person was obedient to his or her parents? Pick one brief incident and create your cartoon strip to show the characteristic in action.

Allow students to display and comment on their cartoons. Now proceed with *Step 4*.

Step 4 (1 minute): Make a transition to the next part of the session by commenting, **The Holy Spirit can build the characteristics of Christ into a Christian's life. He produces the fruit of** the Spirit as part of His ministry in the believer's life. This fruit includes "love, joy, peace, patience, kindness, goodness, faithfulness, gentleness and self-control" (Gal. 5:22,23). While the Spirit's work in believers' lives is supernatural, it does require some cooperation on the part of the Christian. Believers cooperate with God's work in their lives when they obey His instructions as found in the Bible. They cooperate when they read the Bible regularly, thus allowing Him to show them the way He wants them to live. They cooperate when they pray regularly, committing their needs to God and inviting Him to lead and guide them. They cooperate when they fellowship with other Christians whose insights and example will encourage them to become more Christlike.

Remember that growth does not take place overnight. Just like physical growth, spiritual growth is gradual. It is a building process. You grow bit by bit, day by day, without realizing it. But when you look back over six months or a year, you realize how far you have come.

Conclusion and Decision

CONCLUSION (5-10 minutes)

Tell your learners, **Find the "Select a Characteristic" section of your Treasure Seeker worksheet. Think back through the characteristics of Christ we have discussed in this session and prayerfully decide on one that you will work on this week. Ask God to make you more like Christ in this area.** Allow students to work.

Now write out one way you will begin to demonstrate the characteristic you have chosen. For example, perhaps you chose the characteristic of gentleness. You realize that you have been pretty rough on your younger sister lately. So one way to demonstrate gentleness would be to take time to play a game of her choice or to read to her a book of her choice, and to do it cheerfully and pleasantly, without criticizing her or being sarcastic.

Close in prayer. Hand out the Fun Page take-home paper.

NOTES

NOTE: The next session, SESSION 10, requires a little extra preparation. See the note under "SESSION PLAN" and the ATTENTION GRABBER on page 121 for details.

In His Steps

Search the Scriptures you have been assigned for
characteristics of Christ. What was He like?

Jesus is:

John 13:34 _____

Mark 6:34 _____

Matthew 11:29 _____

John 14:31 _____

Luke 2:51 _____

1 Timothy 1:16 _____

Luke 23:34 _____

SESSION 9

Select a Characteristic

Select a characteristic of Christ's from the above list and
write it in the blank.

I've found that Jesus was _____

Now write a specific thing that you will try to do to be
more like Him. For instance, "patience" might be the
characteristic. You could stop yelling at your brother for
messing up your room with his jellyfish collection.

I will start being like Christ by _____

_____

_____

CRUNCHED CHARACTERISTICS!

Hey, a little help! We were trying to invent a word game about some of the great characteristics of Jesus—characteristics like **kind, trusty** and so on. But our typewriter went berserk and mixed up all the words. Your job is to fix the words, like this: split each word in the list below into two parts, and then stick each front part together with the proper back part to form the correct words. For example: the nonsense words **kinsty** and **trud** can be split apart into **kin, sty, tru,** and **d.** They can be reassembled to form **kind** and **trusty.** Sound hard to do? Maybe so! If you need help, the proper words appear in bold letters in the verses below. But try not to peek if you can help it!

LOBLE

COMPENCE

HUMIENT

GENIVE

OBEDASSION

PATIVE

FORGTLE

"As I have loved you, so you must **love** one another." John 13:34

"When Jesus . . . saw a large crowd, he had **compassion** on them." Mark 6:34

"Take my yoke upon you and learn from me, for I am **gentle** and **humble** in heart, and you will find rest for your souls." Matthew 11:29

"If you obey my commands, you will remain in my love, just as I have obeyed my Father's commands and remain in His love." John 15:10. (The word is **obedient.**)

"Christ Jesus might display his unlimited **patience** as an example for those who would believe on him and receive eternal life." 1 Timothy 1:16

"Father, **forgive** them, for they do not know what they are doing." Luke 23:34

DAILY NUGGETS

Wisdom from God's Word for you to read each day.

Day 1 Read John 15:1-8. Who is the "true vine"?

Day 2 John 15:2. Have you felt the bite of the Father's pruning shears?

Day 3 John 15:3, 4. A branch broken off the vine cannot bear fruit, because it is cut off from the source of life. Remember that our ability to bear spiritual fruit (good actions, accomplishments, and so on) does not lie in ourselves, but in Jesus.

Day 4 John 15:5. Who are the branches? How do they bear fruit?

Day 5 John 15:6, 7. How can you avoid being thrown in the rubbish heap?

Day 6 John 15:8. Why is the Father glorified when the disciples of Jesus bear much fruit?

Here's one you should never forget!

Hot Shot

"**Be imitators of God, therefore, as dearly loved children.**"
Ephesians 5:1

The seven characteristics above are seven characteristics you can have if you make a habit of imitating Jesus. The word *Christian* originally meant "little Christ." And that's how we should behave!

POP SHEET

THEME: To become more Christlike, we must *do* the things we say we believe.

BIBLE STUDY OUTLINE:

Read the Parable of the Good Samaritan (found in Luke 10:30-37) with your students. Highlight these points as time permits:

- Jesus expects us to *live* our faith; to put our beliefs into practice every day. The Good Samaritan gives us an illustration of one who rose above the accepted standard of hate and bigotry. The beaten man was a Jew. The Jews and Samaritans were sworn enemies.
- Yet it was the Samaritan who stopped and aided the beaten man, not the Jewish religious leader (the priest), or the Jewish religious associate (the Levite). It is not good enough to wear priestly garments or a pious smile; it's our *actions* that count. The priest and the Levite were certainly both very religious men. But it was the Samaritan whom Jesus held out as a great example of a godly person, because he lived his faith. He put his beliefs into practice.
- This same principle holds today: if we want to be the kind of Christian God wants, we must prove our faith by our actions. *Talk* gives an indication of our ideas, but actions demonstrate our convictions. If we wish to become more and more like Jesus (and don't forget, we don't just stand still; we either become more and more like Him, or we become less and less like Him), we must do the things we say we believe.

OBJECT LESSON: GOD HOLDS US RESPONSIBLE FOR OUR ACTIONS

Materials needed: A tame, friendly pet such as a kitten, puppy, or turtle; a box or carrying case.

Introduce the pet to the group. Continue to hold the pet as you relate the following ideas (if the animal becomes restless, put it in its box or cage):

In some ways, we humans are like this animal. For example, it and we all can see, hear, and feel hunger. But there are many differences too—people don't walk on four legs, animals don't use telephones, and most people don't crave pet food!

One major difference between people and animals is that people are responsible for their actions. A cat or dog or horse is not capable of being held responsible. If a dog bites someone, the injured person doesn't take the dog to court. He takes the owner. Society holds people responsible not only for the actions of their pets, but also for their own actions.

God, too, holds people responsible. We are responsible for our actions and the consequences of those actions. God has placed the responsibility of obeying His laws, and the consequences of disobedience, on each of us. We are each responsible to behave as God wants us to behave.

DISCUSSION QUESTIONS:

1. **Why do you suppose the Samaritan man was so good to the Jewish man?**
2. **How is it possible for a religious person like the priest or Levite to behave so wrongly?**
3. **Is it possible for a person to know all *about* God but not *know Him*?**
4. **If someone in this group asked you what it means to be "godly" or "Christlike," what would you say?**
5. **How does Romans 14:12 ("So then, each of us will give an account of himself to God") relate to this discussion? Is anyone an exception to this verse? How does the idea of judgment—being held responsible for your behavior—make you feel?**

How many things can be done with balloons?

"BALLOON BOOGIE"

For two or more teams. Place a couple dozen slightly underinflated balloons out on the floor. At a signal, one player from each team hops out onto the floor on one foot, holding the other foot up behind with one hand. Players each try to hop on a balloon and pop it. As each player succeeds, he or she runs back to the team so that the next teammate can go. First team to finish wins.

"WALKING ON AIR"

Tie balloons to players' feet and let them hold balloons as shown. Players have time trials or races to see who can cross the finish line without a flat.

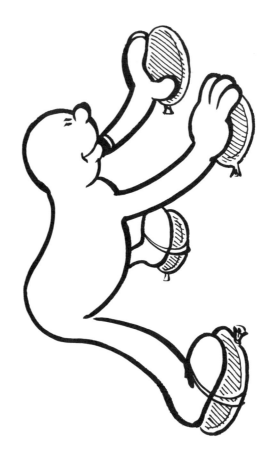

ALSO:

1. Allow all students to have a concert. Students blow up balloons and make sound effects with the escaping air.
2. For outdoors and old clothes: have a water balloon fight with balloons filled with diluted food coloring. Buy large bottles of coloring at a wholesale restaurant supply company.
3. Students vie to see how many balloons they can stuff down their own shirts or blouses.

Love

WHAT THE SESSION IS ABOUT

Love for each other is a mark that identifies Christians.

SCRIPTURE STUDIED

Luke 5:12,13; 6:27-35; 22:50,51; 23:33,34.

KEY PASSAGE

"A new commandment I give you: Love one another. As I have loved you, so you must love one another. All men will know that you are my disciples if you love one another."
John 13:34,35

AIMS OF THE SESSION

During this session your learners will:

1. Describe at least three ways in which Jesus demonstrated His love.
2. List ways they can show love for others.
3. Identify a specific way they will demonstrate love this week.

INSIGHTS FOR THE LEADER

This session focuses on the mark by which Christians should be identifiable: love for one another. The Lord Jesus said that people would recognize His disciples because of this love (see John 13:34,35).

The kind of love our Lord was talking about is a sacrificing love that puts others before itself. This love is not natural; it goes against the human grain.

Young children tend to be self-centered; they may please others when they can benefit, too, but they are not often willing to help others at their own personal expense. Junior highers are beginning to grow out of this childhood point of view. As they grow spiritually they begin to discover what biblical love is—not just a pleasant emotion, but a condition of the will that results in actions that benefit the one who is loved. As one youth pastor once said, "Love is spelled G-I-V-E."

Love is not self-centered; it looks to the needs of others. Read Luke 6:27-36, the main passage your students will study. A few of the highlights include:

Love for Hate

"But I tell you who hear me: Love your enemies, do good to those who hate you" (vs. 27). As Jesus hinted in this verse, love is *doing good*.

Christians are to do good even to those who hate us. We not only have the Lord's words to that effect, we have His example. He did good, He practiced what He preached. In Luke 22:47-51, for instance, Jesus healed the ear of a slave who was part of the crowd that came to capture Jesus and eventually crucify Him.

Junior high students will rarely have the opportunity to heal the ear of an enemy, but perhaps they might fill the ear of an unfriendly acquaintance with kind advice and overtures of friendship. Or they may speak kindly of an unpopular student. These are practical acts of Christian love that could help "heal" another person.

Blessings for Curses

"Bless those who curse you, pray for those who mistreat you" (vs. 28). Jesus did these very things while He hung on the cross. He prayed, "Father, forgive them, for they do not know what they are doing" (see Luke 23:34).

Praying for another is an act of love, as is blessing others. Your students should be in the habit of praying for their friends—and their enemies. You may wish to stress the importance of prayer during class time. It is a wonderful and rewarding privilege that should be developed early in one's Christian life.

Turn the Other Cheek

"If someone strikes you on one cheek, turn to him the other also" (Luke 6:29). When His

jailors struck Him, recorded in Luke 22:63,64, Jesus could easily have used divine powers to punish them. But He didn't. Our imaginations can dwell on the drama that occurred in that room. Pained and grieved, Jesus turned His cheek.

While junior high age people are sometimes prone to physically "duke it out" behind the school, most students will never be called upon to literally turn a cheek to fists. However, all of your students have probably faced the emotional pain of spurned friendship or other traumas. Turning the cheek—giving the "enemy" a second chance rather than exploding in rage or seething with hatred—is the Christlike thing to do. Many a strong relationship has been formed when one young person smiles at another who has frowned at him.

Lend Without Return

"Lend to them without expecting to get anything back. Then your reward will be great, and you will be sons of the Most High, because he is kind to the ungrateful and wicked" (Luke 6:35).

Jesus lived up to this statement, too. Knowing He would receive no financial reward or return favor, Jesus healed a leper (see Luke 5:12,13). Lepers were considered unclean and were forced to dwell in abject poverty outside the city limits. The act of touching the sick man sent a powerful message of love and kindness to all who witnessed the event.

This, of course, is just one example from Christ's ministry. He spent His entire public life helping those who could not repay. We owe our very salvation to Him, but the debt we owe is beyond our means to repay. The only way to return even a fraction of the favor is to obey His words and to live a life focused on Him.

When Jesus told us to lend and give without hope of repayment, He meant that we are to help the helpless. It's easy to help people we like. It's easy to help those who will likely someday help us. But it can be a whole new and wonderful experience to give to those who cannot give in return. Your students can take an important stand for Christ in their circles of friends by "sticking up for the underdog"—the unpopular or ostracized person—or by assisting the poor, aged, infirm, or imprisoned.

Love in Action

People have many needs today—physical, emotional, social. Junior highers need to be aware of their responsibility to help meet other people's needs in a real, practical way. This may involve the sacrifice of money, time or effort. It might mean baby-sitting for someone with many children but little money. It might mean mowing the lawn for the older woman next door after doing one's own lawn. It might mean trying to make friends with a new kid in school or with someone whom others have avoided because of appearance or a handicap.

Love is not easy. It means giving up our own ideas and letting God fill us with His ideas for helping other people. That's why love is the mark of a Christian, the way to identify true disciples of Jesus Christ. It can only occur in those who are empowered by God Himself.

SESSION PLAN

BEFORE CLASS BEGINS: On a sheet of note paper, list six to ten famous ad slogans which your students are likely to recognize.

Attention Grabber

ATTENTION GRABBER (3-5 minutes)

Tell students that you are about to challenge them with a fun guessing game. Say, **The object of this game is for you to identify famous advertising slogans and the products or companies they represent. I will say the first word of the slogan. If you think you can guess the entire slogan, raise your hand and I will call on you. If nobody can guess correctly, I will say the second word of the slogan and so on until someone identifies the answer.**

Choose one of the best known slogans on your list to start the game. An example of a famous slogan and how you would read it as students guess is shown here:

"You . . . "
"You deserve . . . "
"You deserve a . . . "
"You deserve a break . . . "

(By this time your students would recognize, "You deserve a break today at McDonald's.")

After your learners have had fun identifying all the slogans on your list, focus on the main point of this session by saying, **Advertising slogans help us to identify various products and their key features. Today we're going to find out that there is a "mark" that identifies Christians.**

CREATIVE OPTION (8-10 minutes)

Assemble your students into two teams on each side of the room. Give the teams alternating turns to guess the slogans—as described above—until someone gives the correct answer. Keep track of the score.

Bible Exploration

EXPLORATION (30-40 minutes)

Step 1 (5-10 minutes): Read John 13:34,35 to your class: **A new commandment I give you: Love one another. As I have loved you, so you must love one another. All men will know that you are my disciples if you love one another.**

Tell students, **Jesus said that people will know we are His disciples if we love each other. That is our mark, the mark of love which identifies us as Christians. Today we are going to look at some examples of the way Jesus loved, and then we will discuss how you and I can show Jesus-style love to the people around us.**

Have students form groups of two to four to work the "Jesus in Action" section of the Treasure Seeker worksheet.

Step 2 (5-7 minutes): Allow time for students to complete worksheets, then go over the answers with them, commenting on the acts of love Jesus performed. (See INSIGHTS FOR THE LEADER for background.) Answers are on the illustration on this page.

Step 3 (10-12 minutes): Assign each group one or more of the case studies listed under "Love in Action" on the worksheet.

Allow students time to work. Say, **I would like one person from each group to share what the group decided about their situation.**

Step 4 (8-10 minutes): Then say, **Now we are going to brainstorm additional ways to show love to the people described in the "Love in Action" section of the Treasure Seeker. Feel**

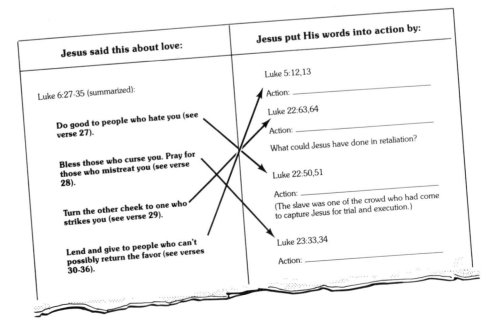

Jesus said this about love:

Jesus put His words into action by:

Luke 6:27-35 (summarized):

Do good to people who hate you (see verse 27).

Bless those who curse you. Pray for those who mistreat you (see verse 28).

Turn the other cheek to one who strikes you (see verse 29).

Lend and give to people who can't possibly return the favor (see verses 30-36).

Luke 5:12,13

Action: _____

Luke 22:63,64

Action: _____
What could Jesus have done in retaliation?

Luke 22:50,51

Action: _____
(The slave was one of the crowd who had come to capture Jesus for trial and execution.)

Luke 23:33,34

Action: _____

free to speak up with any ideas you have. Remember, in brainstorming no one is allowed to criticize another person's idea.

Take the situations from the Treasure Seeker one by one and let students brainstorm ways to show love to the person described. Jot their answers on the chalkboard. Here are some ideas to share if students need help. In the case of Morton the Klutz, a loving person would work with him and try to help him improve. Love would give him an opportunity to practice, and would put up with his clumsy efforts even if it meant losing points. Love would stand its ground in defending Morton's right to participate.

In the case of Zelda, the unpopular girl, a loving person would be unselfish and would make room in his or her life for Zelda. Love would befriend her, spend time with her, let her talk about her problems, and try to help her become more self-confident so that she would fit in better with the others at school.

In the case of the little brother, love for the brother and for the mother will prompt a person to take Junior along. Love will also pay attention to the brother and give him an opportunity to participate and to feel valued; love will not complain about having to take him, or begrudge his presence, even though there is disappointment at having to change plans.

Conclusion and Decision

CONCLUSION (2-3 minutes)

Draw students' attention to the "Kindness Kard" on the student worksheet. Tell them to work individually to think of a good way to put love into action for a specific person. Let students know that they don't have to actually give the card away, but they should perform the loving action.

Close in prayer and distribute the Fun Page.

CREATIVE ALTERNATIVE (2-3 minutes)

Gather students into pairs, girls with girls and boys with boys. (If there is an odd number of students, you sit with the extra person.) Tell learners to discuss and decide upon specific acts of kindness that they will do for each other this week. To stimulate thinking, suggest that they consider actions such as sharing lunches at school, introducing each other to their "crowds," calling each other on the phone, going to a movie together, and so on.

NOTE: The next session requires a page of want ads from your local newspaper.

Jesus in Action

When Jesus spoke of love, He put His words into action. Read what Jesus said about love in Luke 6:27-35 (summarized in the column on the left below). Then read the verses listed in the column on the right, drawing lines to connect what Jesus said to appropriate examples of what He did to back up His words.

Jesus said this about love:	Jesus put His words into action by:
Luke 6:27-35 (summarized):	Luke 5:12,13
	Action: _____
Do good to people who hate you (see verse 27).	Luke 22:63,64
	Action: _____
Bless those who curse you. Pray for those who mistreat you (see verse 28).	What could Jesus have done in retaliation?
	Luke 22:50,51
Turn the other cheek to one who strikes you (see verse 29).	Action: _____
	(The slave was one of the crowd who had come to capture Jesus for trial and execution.)
Lend and give to people who can't possibly return the favor (see verses 30-36).	Luke 23:33,34
	Action: _____

Love in Action

Keep in mind the things Jesus said and did as you work together to answer these questions.

SITUATION #1:

Morton is in your gym class. Everyone puts him down because he can't catch, run, or throw well. You have been elected captain of your team—you also have Morton on your team. The other guys want Morton to sit out the game on the bench. They figure he'll cause the team to lose if he plays, and he may.

1. What should you do when the guys put Morton down?

2. What will you do with Morton?

3. What could you do to encourage him?

SITUATION #2:

Zelda has problems, lots of them. The biggest one is that she is lonely (probably because she doesn't fit in too well with the rest of the kids). You want to be popular and hang around with well-liked people.

1. What could you do to encourage Zelda?

2. What advice could you give her?

SITUATION #3:

Your little brother is always wanting to tag along. It makes him feel important. You are planning to go play ball with some friends. Your mom is going to have company and wants you to take Junior with you.

1. How should you act toward your brother?

2. How could you make him feel important?

Kindness Kard

Think of a specific loving action you could do this week for someone you know. Fill in the blanks on the card.

KINDNESS KARD

Dear _____

This card entitles you to one free act of kindness! I promise I will:

_____

_____

Love, _____

FUN page!

KINDNESS RATE-O-MATIC!

Are you a nice, kind person—or a self-centered slob? Find out fast with the:

Place your pencil point on the "START" below. Beginning with question #1, answer each question yes or no. (Answer honestly—not what you think the answer *should* be, but what you would *actually* do.) Use your pencil to follow the path that your answers will lead you on. Your path will go higher and higher until you reach the top level, where you will find your "Kindness Rating." A sample path has been traced for you in gray.

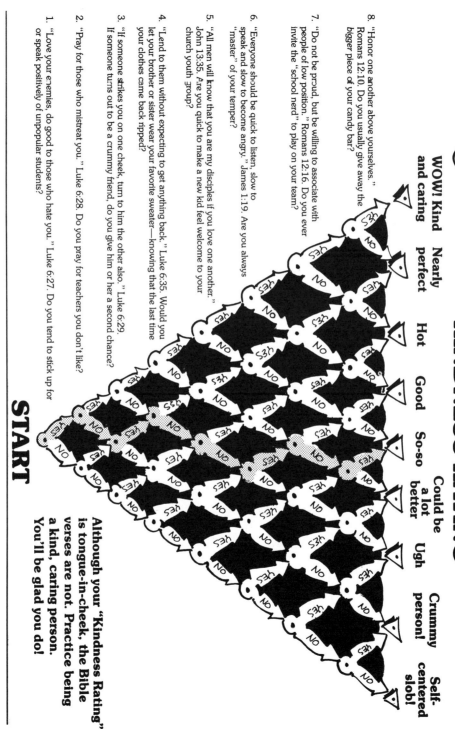

KINDNESS RATING

WOW! Kind and caring — Nearly perfect

Hot

Good

Could be a lot better — So-so

Ugh

Crummy person!

Self-centered slob!

START

Although your "Kindness Rating" is tongue-in-cheek, the Bible verses are not. Practice being a **kind, caring person.** You'll be glad you do!

---

1. "Love your enemies, do good to those who hate you." Luke 6:27. Do you tend to stick up for or speak positively of unpopular students?

2. "Pray for those who mistreat you." Luke 6:28. Do you pray for teachers you don't like?

3. "If someone strikes you on one cheek, turn to him the other also." Luke 6:29. If someone turns out to be a crummy friend, do you give him or her a second chance?

4. "Lend to them without expecting to get anything back." Luke 6:35. Would you let your brother or sister wear your favorite sweater—knowing that the last time your clothes came back ripped?

5. "All men will know that you are my disciples if you love one another." John 13:35. Are you quick to make a new kid feel welcome to your church youth group?

6. "Everyone should be quick to listen, slow to speak and slow to become angry." James 1:19. Are you always "master" of your temper?

7. "Do not be proud, but be willing to associate with people of low position." Romans 12:16. Do you ever invite the "school nerd" to play on your team?

8. "Honor one another above yourselves." Romans 12:10. Do you usually give away the bigger piece of your candy bar?

DAILY NUGGETS

Wisdom from God's Word for you to read each day.

Day 1 Read 1 John 4:7. Where do we get the love that we need to share with others?

Day 2 1 John 4:9,10. How does God show His love to us?

Day 3 1 John 4:11. Because God loved us, we should do what?

Day 4 1 John 4:12,13. The Holy Spirit tells us of God's love and assures us we are in a vital relationship with Him. How have you experienced the effects of God living in you?

Day 5 1 John 4:14-16. Think about the meaning of "God is love." It means more

than if it simply said, "God is *loving*." Can you figure out the difference?

Day 6 1 John 4:20,21. Check up on yourself: are you loving your Christian brothers and sisters? By what actions are you demonstrating your love?

"All men will know that you are my disciples if you love one another." John 13:35

POP SHEET

THEME: Love for each other is a mark that identifies Christians.

CASE STUDY:
THE LOVE OF CHRIST DEMONSTRATED

Begin your message by quoting John 13:34,35: "A new commandment I give you: Love one another. As I have loved you, so you must love one another. By this all men will know that you are my disciples, if you love one another."

Tell your students the following true story:

The small twelve-year old girl was new to the group. She still had her "baby pudge" figure and an awkward manner. Nearly everyone managed to ignore her as she threw her belongings into the van. She slipped into the backseat as the group piled into vehicles for the camp-out. Silence was her companion until Cindy leaned over the seat and began a conversation. "Hi, I'm Cindy," she said cheerfully. "Who are you? Are you new here?" the 13-year old Cindy soon had the little girl talking and adding to the general roar in the van.

Late that night, as the campers were curled up in their warm sleeping bags, the youth director stepped lightly over the scattered snoring bodies for one last check. A head peeped out of a sleeping bag and whispered, "Hey, did you know Cindy doesn't have a sleeping bag?"

"You're kidding!" the youth director exclaimed. "She'll wake up a Popsicle."

The already exhausted director walked on until he spotted a skinny girl huddled and shivering in her jacket on the frosty grass. "Cindy, how could you forget your sleeping bag? Only a Dodo would forget that."

She lifted her head and very quietly responded, "Well, I didn't forget my sleeping bag; I just loaned it to someone who forgot hers." A pudgy face looked timidly out of a bag a couple of feet away.

Cindy had willingly given all the warmth she could offer to a kid no one else really cared about. The youth director produced a spare bag he kept for such occasions and went to bed amazed.

Cindy's generosity is an example of Christ's love shared!

BIBLE STUDY OUTLINE:

Now read Philippians 2:3-8 to your listeners, making the following observations as time permits:
- This passage commands us to have an attitude. The attitude is Christ's; namely, hold others in high regard and always look out for their needs and interests.
- Christ demonstrated this attitude by becoming a servant (see verse 7), becoming a man—feeling what we feel, going through what we go through—and dying for us on a cross (see verse 8).
- This attitude that Christ demonstrated and that we are supposed to practice is what Jesus was talking about in John 13:34,35: love.
- Love is being a servant to others; that is, helping those who need help—such as a kind word or a warm sleeping bag. Love is feeling what another person feels and going through what they go through. Love is caring when no one else cares.

DISCUSSION QUESTIONS:

1. **Why do you suppose Cindy was so generous to the new girl?**
2. **Why did the youth director go to bed amazed?**
3. **Is this sort of generosity the norm among Christians? Why or why not?**
4. **If Jesus had been there to talk to Cindy, what do you think He would have said to her?**
5. **If Jesus were here to talk to us, what do you think He would say to us?**
6. **What are some simple, practical ways a person could put other people first here at this meeting?**

THE COMPLETE JUNIOR HIGH
BIBLE STUDY RESOURCE
BOOK #1

Christian love often gives us a warm feeling. Here are some games that will leave your students cold. To play these games you'll need access to a freezer or ice chest.

"ICE CUBE MELTDOWN"

A game invented generations ago, probably by the ice box companies. Assemble two teams. Each team gets a large block of ice. Object of the game is to be the first team to completely melt the ice by sitting on it. Players take turns sitting on the ice; use a watch to time one minute intervals for each player. Players rotate through as many turns as necessary.

"ESKIMO RELAY"

This one can be played with shirts on, but it's best played at the beach or pool with swimsuits only. Each of two teams has its members pair up. Carrying a cold bag of frozen peas or corn as shown, they attempt to work their way to the finish line. Those who drop the bag must start over. It's hard—if a couple just can't do it, give the next players a chance.

"BOBBING FOR ICE CUBES"

Just like a bobbing for apple game, only the apples are ice cubes and the water is freezing cold.

"ICE CUBE BREATH"

A good game for both team and individual competition. The object is to see how fast individuals can transfer a pile of ice cubes to a bucket nearby. Contestants can only use their mouths to handle the ice cubes.

Friends

WHAT THE SESSION IS ABOUT

The choice of close friends is very important to Christians.

SCRIPTURE STUDIED

Proverbs 18:24; Romans 13:12; 1 Corinthians 13:7; 15:33; Galatians 6:2; 1 John 2:10.

KEY PASSAGE

"Do two walk together unless they have agreed to do so?" Amos 3:3

AIMS OF THE SESSION

During this session, your learners will:
1. Examine the importance of, and the biblical basis for, choosing friends.
2. Describe actions that would illustrate biblical concepts regarding friends.
3. Examine their present choices of friends in light of the Scripture study.

INSIGHTS FOR THE LEADER

In the junior high world few things take higher priority than friends. Even though all of us need close relationships, the junior high age seems to feel the greatest need for the acceptance and warmth of a close friend. Although the Bible gives a record of some great friendships, such as David and Jonathan, Ruth and Naomi, Jesus and His disciples, and Paul and Timothy, it puts more stress on the characteristics a friend should or should not possess.

Every student will be able to quickly identify **negative qualities** that would torpedo a friendship. A person who lies or makes up tales (see Prov. 12:13) will quickly be put on the least desirable list. Romans 3:13,14 tells us that bitter or poisonous talk is a trait that does not typify God's people. We are better to stay away from friends who have not "put on the armor of light" (Rom. 13:12) and who, because of a lack of moral and spiritual convictions, often end up "partying," becoming sexually loose and deteriorating to fighting and jealousy (see Rom. 13:13). The Scripture teaches that "Bad company corrupts good character" (1 Cor. 15:33).

Although some young people think that they are an island and can be totally independent, most will agree that they become like the people they spend time with. Although a Christian may not join in with everything his non-Christian friends are doing, spending time with them increases the intensity of temptation.

God realizes that we all need friends. **He wants us to have the best possible kind of friends.** So He has provided some guidelines that produce the best kind of human relationships possible. These produce "a friend who sticks closer than a brother" (Prov. 18:24, *NASB*).

First of all, friends need to agree on important things. Amos wrote "Do two walk together unless they have agreed to do so?" (Amos 3:3). It is important to be in agreement on spiritual things. Those who trust in Christ and those who want no part in Him may have a difficult time getting along. When it comes to decisions reflecting spiritual matters, values and ethics, they are likely to have conflict. In 2 Corinthians 6:14 Paul says not to be unequally yoked with unbelievers. A Christian friendship offers the possibility of lasting unity.

Other characteristics that Christians need to look for in others are found in Galatians 6:2—"Carry each other's burdens"—and 1 Corinthians 13:7—"Always protects, always trusts, always hopes, always perseveres." A friend is supportive, and willing to stick with you even in difficult times. A friend who "lives in the light" (1 John 2:10)—who knows Jesus and who lives according to His commands—can be of great value when we are feeling discouraged or defeated. Having someone who believes in us when we don't feel very good about ourselves is a great encouragement.

NOTES

Having a friend who prays for us and helps us maintain our Christian walk is far better than a friend who tries to erode our faith.

Students should be aware that **friendships are not one-sided.** We must be willing to help our friends, to stand by them, to trust them. We must be willing to forgive our friends if they do something that disturbs us. Colossians 3:13 instructs us to forgive others just as the Lord forgives us. All the qualities that we seek in a friend are qualities that we should attempt to build into our own lives as we walk with the Lord.

In the end we become like our friends, or we lose them. It is much better to surround ourselves with friends who will support us in our Christian life, rather than those who will make it more difficult.

(Note: This session is focused primarily on encouraging your students to select their closest friends on the basis of biblical standards, with a preference for Christians. Adults recognize the importance of befriending non-Christians in order to win them to Jesus, and this course has stressed imitating or modeling Christ as one way of witnessing. Your young people will naturally have many non-Christian friends and acquaintances through school and other activities. However, junior highers are more easily influenced by unsuitable close friends than are adults, and they will seize on any excuse to maintain friendships with such people. Therefore, the editors recommend that you stress the need for developing close friendships with Christian young people, rather than encouraging students to be close friends with worldly kids in order to win them. As your students grow up in years and in Christian maturity, they will be better able to handle closer relationships with worldly people.)

SESSION PLAN

BEFORE CLASS BEGINS: Obtain a page of want ads from your local newspaper.

Attention Grabber

ATTENTION GRABBER (5-7 minutes)

Tell students, **On your Treasure Seeker worksheet you will find a list of qualities that a friend might have. Select five that you consider the most important and list them on the blank lines. Then number your list to indicate the order of importance. Mark "1" by the quality that is most important to you, "2" for the next one, and so on.**

Allow time for students to complete the assignment. Then ask for volunteers to share qualities they have marked number 1, number 2, and number 3. Ask why each quality is important and why they have ranked them in the order they have chosen.

Make a transition to the next part of the session by saying something like this: **Close friendships are very important to all of us. Because God knows this, He has given us some guidance in**

His Word that will help us choose friends who will help us, rather than hinder us, in our lives. Today we're going to look at some of the things He has to say.

Bible Exploration

EXPLORATION (25-35 minutes)

Step 1 (10-12 minutes): Have students form two or more groups of up to six members and appoint a group reporter for each group (select students who are able to read and write well.) Explain, **Look on your Treasure Seeker for the "Match Up" section. Half of you will be looking for good qualities in a friend, and half of you for bad qualities. Look up the Scripture and decide what it says about the qualities you are looking for. Write the statements in the appropriate column on your worksheet.** Assign half the groups to look for good qualities and half to look for bad qualities. Let students work.

Step 2 (6-8 minutes): Regain the attention of the

class and ask for reports from the groups. As the various good and bad qualities are identified, lead a discussion, drawing from the INSIGHTS FOR THE LEADER and using questions such as these: **How would you feel about having a friend whose word you couldn't trust because he lied a lot? Would you enjoy a friend who always had something bitter to say? Do you think it's a good idea to spend a lot of time with someone who is always fighting? What do you think a "friend who sticks closer than a brother" would be like? Would you enjoy having a friend who always thought the best of you, and who was patient with your faults?**

Step 3 (4-5 minutes): Read sample want ads from your local newspaper. Then say, **Now you are going to write a "want ad" for a friend. Work individually to select three good scriptural qualities you would like a friend to have. Then create an advertisement in which you list characteristics.**

Step 4 (5-10 minutes): Have several volunteers share their ads and explain why they selected the characteristics they did. Summarize by saying something like this: **We have seen that there are many qualities that make a good friend, and many that make an undesirable friend. God wants us all to have the best possible friendships, but we have to do our part by being discerning about the people we choose as friends, and by developing the qualities of a good friend in ourselves.**

NOTES

Conclusion and Decision

CONCLUSION (8-10 minutes)

Say, **Look at the section on your worksheet where you are asked to list your five closest friends. Write their initials. Put your closest friend's name beside the number 1, the next closest person beside number two, and so on. Then decide if they have some of the qualities of a good friend we have discussed. If they do, put a plus sign next to their initials.**

Allow time for students to complete the assignment. Then regain their attention by asking,

What has your list told you about your choice of friends? How do your friends compare with the list of five important qualities you made at the beginning of class? Think about it silently for a moment. Then spend a moment in prayer asking for God's guidance in your friendships.

Close in prayer. Distribute the Fun Page take-home paper.

NOTE: The next session requires a number of advertisements cut from magazines, and 3″ × 5″ cards. See pages 144 and 146 for details.

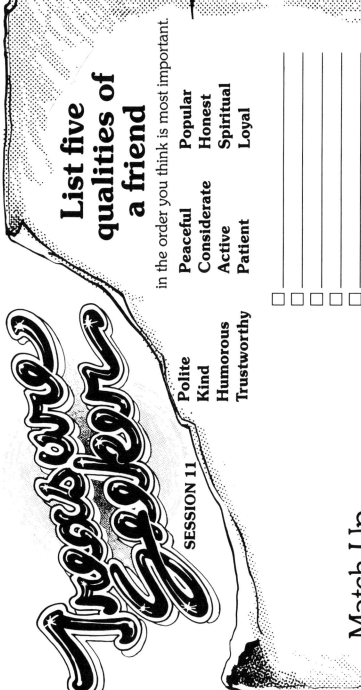

List five qualities of a friend

in the order you think is most important.

Polite	Peaceful	Popular
Kind	Considerate	Honest
Humorous	Active	Spiritual
Trustworthy	Patient	Loyal

☐ _____

☐ _____

☐ _____

☐ _____

☐ _____

Match Up

Figure out what characteristics are good and bad for a friend to have and list the characteristics in the appropriate boxes.

Prov. 11:13
Prov. 18:24
Ecc. 4:9
Amos 3:3
Rom. 3:13,14
Rom. 13:9
Rom. 13:12,13
1 Cor. 13:7
1 Cor. 15:33
2 Cor. 6:14
Gal. 5:22
Gal. 6:2
Col. 3:13
1 John 2:10

GOOD	BAD

My five closest friends are:

Give initials

1.
2.
3.
4.
5.

If these friends have some scriptural qualities of a good friend, give a " + " next to initials.

HOW MANY FRIENDS CAN YOU FIND?

Starting at Herschel Snodgrass below, use a pencil to trace the route with the largest number of friends (the little stick figures). End up in the "Close Circle of Friends" at the top. Award yourself one point for each friend you find. Rules: You cannot use the same section of path twice, and you can't cross your own path except on strings that don't touch.

Close Circle of Friends

Herschel Snodgrass

SCORE:

22—Bad!
24-28—OK
32 or more—GREAT!

In real life it takes more than a pencil and a few minutes of time to find true friends. We could give you all kinds of suggestions for winning friends, but all our advice can be summed up in one thought: **Be like Jesus. Imitate His love, kindness, integrity, and so on. You'll have more friends than you know what to do with!**

DAILY NUGGETS

Day 1   Read Acts 9:26-28. (The "he" in these verses is Paul, also known as Saul.) How was Barnabas a friend to Paul? How did Barnabas' actions help God work?

Day 2   Acts 18:24-28. How were Priscilla and Aquila friends to Apollos? How did their actions help God's work?

Day 3   John 15:14. What does it take to be Jesus' friend?

Day 4   Matthew 8:5-13. How was the centurion a friend to his slave? What was the result?

Day 5   Acts 10:22,23,34-48. How had this centurion been a friend to the Jews? What happened to him?

Day 6   James 4:4. Which would you rather be friends with, the world or God?

Walk this one into your memory.

"Do two walk together unless they have agreed to do so?"

Amos 3:3

THE COMPLETE JUNIOR HIGH BIBLE STUDY RESOURCE BOOK #1
© 1987 GL/LIGHT FORCE, VENTURA, CA 93006

THEME: The choice of close friends is very important to a Christian.

BIBLE STUDY OUTLINE:

Read Mark 2:1-12, the story of the paralyzed man who was taken to Jesus, to your listeners. As time allows, cover these points:

- Jesus was extremely popular at this time. He had the words of truth and life. People today still desperately seek for the answers Jesus provides. There are people in this room who need to crowd in next to Jesus.
- The friends who carried the paralyzed man showed incredible faith.
- They so strongly felt that Jesus could help, they ruined the roof of the house!
- The stretcher bearers wouldn't let the crowd stand in the way of their love for their friends or their faith in Jesus. How many of us allow the attitudes and the opinions of the crowd to stand in the way of our Christian life?
- Imagine the reaction of the crowd when they saw first a beam of light, then a stream of dust and plaster falling around Jesus as He spoke! Everyone must have looked up to see eyes peering down through the hole. Next came the paralytic himself. What would **our** crowd do now if it saw Christians with that much faith?
- Though the man came to be physically healed, Christ first took care of his spiritual problem. The forgiveness of sin is perhaps the most important thing that happens when a person meets Christ.
- Jesus demonstrated His authority to deal with the spiritual sickness by healing the man's physical problem. Christ still has that same power and desire to help us today. We merely need to come to Him.

CASE STUDY: FRIENDS

Begin this case study by saying something like, **I am not only impressed by the faith of these men, I am very moved by their friendship for the paralyzed man. Right now I want to tell you a true story about a young guy named Clint, who had some problems with friends.**

In your own words tell the story of Clint, a young man who was very unsure of himself. He was the smallest kid in the class and he had been in nine schools in 12 years. His father was in the armed forces and their family moved almost every year.

Clint was quiet and reserved. It was very difficult for him to make friends because he didn't want to get close only to experience the pain of another move.

In one of Clint's low moments, he poured out his heart to his school counselor. "I'm short and I hate being short. I don't have any friends. I hate moving and it looks like we'll have to move again next year."

DISCUSSION QUESTIONS:

1. **If you were Clint, what would you need or want to hear?**
2. **What could Clint do to help make friends where he lived?**
3. **If you were such a friend as one of the stretcher bearers, what would you do to help Clint?**
4. **How can Christ help us each be a better friend to our friends?**
5. **What are some of the characteristics of a good friend?**
6. **What are some of the things you *wouldn't* want to see in a friend?**
7. **Do you think it's important to Christ that we wisely pick our friends? Why?**

THE COMPLETE JUNIOR HIGH
BIBLE STUDY RESOURCE
BOOK #1

**Dress up your group with these
fashionable games.**

"CLOTHES HOG"

This game requires a great deal of old clothes. A perfect "bait" for a youth group clothing drive.

For two or more teams. Each team elects a volunteer to dress. Object of the game is to put the largest number of clothing articles on the volunteer during a three minute time limit. Shirts and pants must be worn as they normally would, but it's not necessary to button all the buttons.

For added fun, see which volunteer can take off all the extra clothes the quickest.

"WHAT A KICK"

Play a regular game of soccer (or a smaller version with a Whiffle-style ball), but participants must wear their shoes on the wrong feet. This makes for some pretty wild shots—not to mention calluses.

Try the shoe-on-the-wrong-foot trick with other games your group likes to play.

"FASHION NEWS"

Award points to the team that can dress a volunteer in the most outrageous costume created with newspapers and tape. Extra points for accessories such as hats, belts, gloves, and shoes.

Influenced by the World

INSIGHTS FOR THE LEADER

WHAT THE SESSION IS ABOUT

Christians need to recognize and combat negative influences of the world.

SCRIPTURE STUDIED

2 Timothy 2:22; 1 Peter 2:11; 2 Peter 1:3; 1 John 4:1.

KEY PASSAGE

"Do not conform any longer to the pattern of this world, but be transformed by the renewing of your mind. Then you will be able to test and approve what God's will is—his good, pleasing and perfect will."
Romans 12:2

AIMS OF THE SESSION

During this session your learners will:
1. Recognize ways people are influenced by the world.
2. Discuss the sources of the worldly influences.
3. Describe ways to filter out the world's messages.

Young people today are the targets of the most powerful array of messages ever assembled on earth. The means of spreading these messages are both widespread and seductive. For example, studies suggest that by the time the average teenager today reaches age 65, he or she will have spent the equivalent of nine years watching TV. This amount of exposure cannot fail to mold a person's thinking. Your students may be able to sing many advertising jingles, while they struggle to recall even one Bible verse. Commercials promote materialism and greed, while television comedies and dramas portray values and life-styles that are often opposed to biblical teachings.

Since it is not practical to cut young people off from all contact with the world, we must teach them how to **resist the impact that the world has on them.** This is the purpose of the Scripture study in this session. It covers a number of verses which suggest ways to handle worldly pressures.

Do Not Love the World

Your students will examine 1 John 2:15-17, which exhorts Christians not to love the world. James 4:4 adds that **being a friend of the world means being an enemy of God.** It is not the world of nature which is meant in these Scriptures, but rather the man-made world system with its cravings, evil desires and materialistic emphasis on possessions. The "world" consists of all the things that tend to separate a person from God—all the things a person might put before God in his or her priorities. The details will differ from person to person. One may be able to enjoy football without letting it interfere with his relationship with the Lord, while another finds the sport so consuming that it takes God's place of prominence in his life. Christian young people need to get their priorities lined up correctly, with God at the top of the list. When He is in first place, He can teach them how to arrange the other elements of life.

Those who put God first will find that they are "aliens and strangers in the world" (1 Pet. 2:11). They are no longer completely at home in this world, because their true home is with God. Thus they "abstain from sinful desires" (v. 11), because these are part of the world's system rather than of God's system.

Students may feel that it is difficult to put God first, but God does not give His children instructions without giving the necessary help in carrying them out. **"His divine power has given us everything we need for life and godliness"** (2 Pet. 1:3). He will help young people who wish to resist the world's influences in order to live for Him.

One of the things Christians need is wisdom, and God has promised to give it in answer to believing prayer (see Jas. 1:5). Christian young people who aren't sure how to

handle the world's influences can come to God confidently and ask for His help and wisdom.

As Christians walk with God, they find that He teaches them more and more about Himself and His kind of living. He remakes their attitudes and creates a new "self" for them (see Eph. 4:22-24). He gives His grace to His children; and in turn, they are to make the effort to be self-controlled and to prepare their minds for acting the way He directs, rather than conforming to their former sinful way of life (see 1 Pet. 1:13,14).

One way in which God gives grace and wisdom is by helping His children **"test the spirits to see whether they are from God"** (1 John 4:1). Students need discernment when they consider the various influences that surround them. Some will be worldly—they will promote selfishness and ungodly living. Others will be of God—they will speak of love and of caring for others. Young people need to test the spirits rather than blindly accepting everything they hear. The world can be extremely attractive, with its sparkle and flash; it offers thrills that young people think are lacking in the Church and in Christian living. Students need help in learning how to monitor the message; they need to be able to filter it, to weigh it against the truth of the Bible.

It is also important to teach them to resist Satan. If they do, Scripture says that he will flee (see Jas. 4:7). Our Lord even provides weapons and armor for His children (see Eph. 6:11-17). He provides everything needed in the battle. God is on the side of the Christian who is standing up against evil, and the devil has to run away from our all powerful Lord.

The final Scripture offers a piece of practical advice: "Flee the evil desires of youth" (2 Tim. 2:22). "Get up and get out" is a simple but effective way of avoiding the world's entrapment. Joseph practiced this method when he fled from Potiphar's wife (see Gen. 39:11,12). It is often the best response to a powerful temptation or a sticky situation, such as a party that is getting out of hand.

Your young people are growing up; they are beginning to learn to weigh ideas and to evaluate the messages that come to them. Encourage them to "test the spirits" and to rely on God for wisdom. Urge them to put Him first in their lives and to allow Him to show them the way to live, rather than allowing the pressures of the world to determine their life-style.

SESSION PLAN

BEFORE CLASS BEGINS: Gather a number of advertisements cut from magazines. You'll also need a stack of 3″ × 5″ cards if using OPTIONAL STEP 4 under EXPLORATION

Attention Grabber

ATTENTION GRABBER (5-10 minutes)

Have students form groups of three; give several magazine ads to each group. Explain, **Look at the ads and decide what claims (subtle or explicit) they make about what the product** will do for those who use it. (For example, it will give you sex appeal or make you a wiser consumer.) Discuss your ideas in your group and be prepared to report to the rest of the class.

Let students work for a few minutes. Then regain their attention and ask for their reports. Discuss the ideas that are promoted in magazine, radio, and TV advertising and the ways people are influenced by these ads.

Focus on the main point of the session by saying, **We are influenced by the world around us every waking hour of every day. Advertisements such as these try to make us choose certain products or ideas. The TV set, the people we know, the stories we read—all influence our thinking and behavior. Much of this influence is negative—against what we Christians know to be right and good.**

Today we are going to take a look at what we can do to combat harmful influences.

Bible Exploration

EXPLORATION (20-45 minutes)

Materials needed (If using optional *Step 4*): enough 3"x5" cards for each student to have two or more.

Step 1 (3-5 minutes): Say, **Look at the Treasure Seeker worksheet. Work on your own to list all the ways shown in the picture in which the influence of the world comes to people. Then list any other ways you can think of that are not in the picture.**

Step 2 (10-15 minutes): Continue by saying, **Now turn to "The Scripture Search Game." Get together with one other person to play the game.** Read the instructions to your students. When you are sure all understand how the game is played, give the signal to begin. When five minutes have passed, tell students to put their pencils down.

Step 3 (5-10 minutes): Ask students what they have found in the Scripture. List their responses on the chalkboard. As you go over the words which the students were supposed to circle in the letter grid, note that words appear in the grid which are *not* supposed to be circled! If students did circle them, points must be subtracted from their scores. Review their findings briefly, supplementing as needed from the INSIGHTS FOR THE LEADER. Stress the main

point that the world is constantly trying to press people into its own mold. Christians need to resist this pressure by spending time with God in the Word and prayer, and letting Him control their thoughts and their lives.

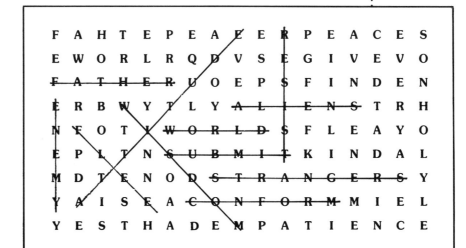

NOTES

OPTIONAL *STEP 4* (10-15 minutes)

Give each student two 3"x5" cards. (If you have only a few learners, give each four cards and have them do the following assignment twice.)

Tell students, **We are going to play a wacky game that can have some silly consequences—but will also teach us how to combat harmful influences. I want you to work individually on this.**

First, on one of your cards write a one- or two-sentence "story" that describes a Christian being confronted with some kind of worldly pressure or influence. For example, "George is offered alcohol at a party" or "Tracy finds a wallet with lots of money and the owner's address. Her greedy friend tells Tracy to keep the loot."

When you've done that, take your second card and write the word "But" in big letters at the top. Then complete the story you have written by describing the proper thing a Christian should do. For example, "But he refused to take a drink" or "But she was honest and returned the wallet."

Allow students a few minutes to complete the assignment (circulate around the room to help students who are stuck). Then collect the cards, keeping the story cards separate from the "But" cards. Shuffle each stack of cards. Draw the top story card and read it aloud. Then draw the top "But" card and read it aloud. Chances are they will not match. They may even sound silly or humorous together. (As you read, change [if necessary] the gender—"he" or "she"—so that both cards match in this aspect.)

After you have read a pair of cards, ask students what the proper Christian response should be and have them suggest Scriptures they have just studied that apply to the situation. Assist the students by suggesting appropriate verses they may not have mentioned. Do this for all cards.

Conclusion and Decision

CONCLUSION (5-10 minutes)

Look again at your list of ways the world influences people. Circle the influence that affects you the most. Then use the extra paper to write a prayer asking for wisdom to deal with the area you circled. If you have any ideas for dealing with it, include them in your prayer.

Close in prayer. As students leave, hand out the Fun Page take-home paper.

How in the World Are You Influenced?

List any other ways you can think of that are not in the picture.

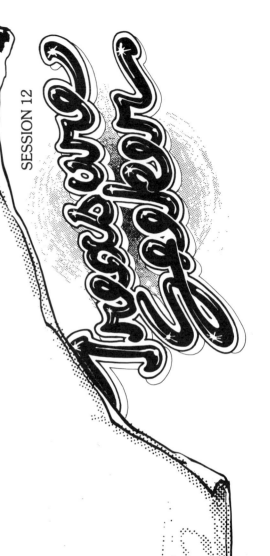

The Scripture Search Game

The object of this game is to complete the assignment before your partner does. You both have exactly five minutes to do so.

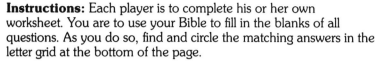

Instructions: Each player is to complete his or her own worksheet. You are to use your Bible to fill in the blanks of all questions. As you do so, find and circle the matching answers in the letter grid at the bottom of the page.

Award yourself five points for each question answered correctly, and one point for each **letter** in the circled words. (The longer the word, the more points it's worth.) Subtract the same number of points for each incorrect answer.

1. According to 1 John 2:15, we should not love the _____ or anything in it.

2. According to 1 John 2:16, the bad influences come from the world, not from the _____.

3. James 4:4 indicates that to be a friend to the world is to be an _____ of God.

4. In 1 Peter 2:11, Christians are referred to as _____ and _____.

5. According to 2 Peter 1:3, God's divine _____ has given us everything we need for life and godliness.

6. James 1:5 tells us that God will give us _____ if we ask for it.

7. According to Ephesians 4:23, we are supposed to be made new in the _____ of our minds.

8. According to 1 Peter 1:14, we are not to _____ to our old evil desires.

9. In 1 John 4:1, we are told to _____ the spirits.

10. James 4:7 tells us that we are to _____ to God and _____ the devil so that he will flee from us.

11. In 2 Timothy 2:22, we are advised to _____ the evil desires (or "youthful lusts").

```
F  A  H  T  E  P  E  A  E  E  R  P  E  A  C  E  S
E  W  O  R  L  R  Q  D  V  S  E  G  I  V  E  V  O
F  A  T  H  E  R  U  O  E  P  S  F  I  N  D  E  N
E  R  B  W  Y  T  L  Y  A  L  I  E  N  S  T  R  H
N  F  O  T  I  W  O  R  L  D  S  F  L  E  A  Y  O
E  P  L  T  N  S  U  B  M  I  T  K  I  N  D  A  L
M  D  T  E  N  O  D  S  T  R  A  N  G  E  R  S  Y
Y  A  I  S  E  A  C  O  N  F  O  R  M  M  I  E  L
Y  E  S  T  H  A  D  E  M  P  A  T  I  E  N  C  E
```

HOW CONFORMED ARE YOU?

You probably realize that the people and things around you tend to influence your thinking and behavior. But to what extent? Too much? Let's find out! Play

Read the situations below. Put a check mark in the box of each one you answer yes. Compare your answers to the "Conformed Rating Sheet."

☐ **1.** Did you make your parents buy you a "Cabbage Patch Kid" when you were younger?

☐ **2.** Do you wear a popular designer brand of clothes even though they cost much more and aren't better made than the look-alike labels?

☐ **3.** Is there someone in your school you would like to date (even if you're too young) and if so, is it because he or she loves Jesus?

☐ **4.** Have you smoked a cigarette?

☐ **5.** Do you feel sorry for the "school nerd" but ignore him because everybody else ignores him?

☐ **6.** Do you fix your hair the way your friends fix theirs even though you know that, on you, it looks stupid?

Conformed Rating Sheet

Box #1. If you checked this box, chances are TV has a great deal of influence upon you. Without television, the Cabbage Patch Kids would have just been another line of ugly dolls.

Box #2. You follow the crowd. You let other people set the style for your thinking and behavior—even if it's not always for the best.

Box #3. You are wise. Many people are attracted to that "special someone" because he or she has a big pool at home or a hot car, good looks or special status—even if he or she is boring and cloddish!

Box #4. You probably smoked because it was "cool"—but disgusting! You may have thought it made you look mature, though it probably made you look green. Most people start smoking, not because it seems pleasant, but because they caved in to crowd pressure.

Box #5. How sad. You give in to the pressure of the crowd, even if it means hurting an underdog.

Box #6. The influence of the world has convinced you that conforming is so important you're willing to ignore your own better judgment.

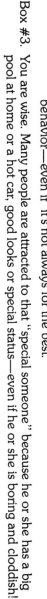

Now that you have taken our test, how did you do? Are you highly conformed to the world—or thinking for yourself? Center your thinking on God. Let Him transform you into an interesting, unique individual!

DAILY NUGGETS

Wisdom from God's Word for you to read each day.

Day 1 Read Romans 3:19. Who does the law speak to? Who is accountable to God?

Day 2 Proverbs 22:24,25. Why is it important not to be close friends with someone who is easily angered?

Day 3 John 15:18,19. Do you belong to the world? If not, to whom do you belong?

Day 4 Mark 8:34-37. What do we lose in gaining the world? Is it worth it?

Day 5 Titus 2:11,12. In today's life of ungodliness and worldly possessions, what does God's grace teach us?

Day 6 1 Corinthians 1:20,21,27. What does God do with the world's wisdom? What pleases God?

Hot Thot

"Do not conform any longer to the pattern of this world, but be transformed by the renewing of your mind. Then you will be able to test and approve what God's will is—his good, pleasing and perfect will."

Romans 12:2

POP SHEET

THEME: The world can negatively influence Christians. God's Word is our protection.

BIBLE STUDY OUTLINE

Tell the story of the wise man who built his house on the rock, found in Matthew 7:24-27. As you make the following points, follow the instructions for the OBJECT LESSON.

- Sand is easy to move. Wind blows it away and rain washes it away. Sand is ever changing and shifting.
- Rock, on the other hand, is hard and solid. It is permanent and lasting.
- A building must be built on a firm foundation if it is to last through years of storms and years of use. (At this point, relate the TRUE STORY.)
- As a house must be built on a firm foundation to survive, we must build our lives on a firm foundation if we expect to withstand life's struggles, hard times, and temptations. Jesus' teaching is the firm foundation, the rock of truth.
- Building our foundation is hard work. We want to get on with our lives. But without a solid foundation in truth, the lives we build have nothing to hold them up.
- In this story Jesus told, storms came even to the strong house. We Christians will experience trials. God never promised we would always have blue skies. But based on God's Word, we can survive anything.

OBJECT LESSON: THE FOUNDATION

Before class, fill a clear plastic bag with sand. Find a large rock.
As you give your talk, show the sand and rock. Refer to them at appropriate times as you talk about building a firm foundation.

TRUE STORY: CARDBOARD CITY

Years ago, before the Baja city of Tijuana built its modern flood control system, there was a huge dry riverbed just outside of town that would fill with flash floods in the rainy season.

Because of the seasonal flooding, no one was foolish enough to buy property for homes in the sandy riverbed. Yet there were homes there, tens of thousands of cardboard shacks made by people too poor to live elsewhere. Every year the shacks would be built, and every year the floods would come and wash them away. Many people would drown and thousands would be left homeless.

But just a few yards away from these pitiful shacks were nice homes up on the strong river bank, homes of wood and stucco and tile, homes built on solid foundations. When the floods came, these places survived.

DISCUSSION QUESTIONS

1. **In verse 24 Jesus talked about hearing and practicing His words. What does He mean by "practicing"?**
2. **Why would someone who practices Jesus' teaching be on a firm foundation?**
3. **What are some of the storms and troubles a person your age might face?**
4. **How could Jesus help with those troubles you just mentioned?**
5. **Is it hard for a person your age to be interested in God's Word? Why or why not?**

THE COMPLETE JUNIOR HIGH
BIBLE STUDY RESOURCE
BOOK #1

Things to do with stuff from the kitchen.

"ARE YOU PEANUTS?"

Using only the spoons in their mouths, teams must dig a glob of peanut butter from a jar and pass it from person to person (spoon to spoon) to the end of the row. First team to do so wins.

"GRAPE GRABBER"

Players attempt to spear grapes from a plate on forks held in their mouths. The person with the most grapes wins. Play for time limit or until grapes are gone.

"BAREFOOT IN THE PARK"

At a signal, two or more teams of several people each remove their socks and stuff them into gallon plastic milk or juice jugs (one jug per team). First team to do so wins. The fun comes when teams are told to be the first to get all their socks back out and on. Surprise! It's not easy. Best when played during the months when kids are likely to wear socks.

"CONDIMENT CALAMITY"

At your next hamburger fry, play this fun little exercise in cooperation.

Hungry participants will be given the opportunity to draw file cards at random, five cards per person. Each file card is labeled with the name of one condiment. The condiments are *lettuce, tomato, catsup, relish, mayonnaise, mustard, pickle, cheese,* and anything else you plan to serve.

When participants pick cards, they may trade with other people for condiments they prefer. They may give cards away even if they don't want anything in return. When all bargaining is through, the cards are traded in for the actual fixings.

The trick is to make several copies of each condiment, but slightly fewer copies than there are participants.

Reviewing "Christian Basics"

INSIGHTS FOR THE LEADER

WHAT THE SESSION IS ABOUT

Scripture from previous sessions

SCRIPTURE STUDIED

A review of Scripture from this course.

KEY PASSAGE

"I have hidden your word in my heart that I might not sin against you." Psalm 119:11

AIMS OF THE SESSION

During this session your learners will:

1. Review themes of the twelve previous sessions of this course.
2. Identify or locate designated Scripture.
3. Identify personal growth that has occurred during this course.

The preceding sessions were designed to provide students with a grasp of some of the elementary ideas and skills of the Christian faith. These concepts are reviewed briefly in the following paragraphs. You may wish to reread the INSIGHTS FOR THE LEADER sections from the other sessions to obtain a more thorough review of the Bible truths found in this course.

The first session introduced the idea of **belief** and of establishing a personal relationship with Jesus Christ. Belief means a commitment, or putting one's trust in Christ. It is demonstrated by the action of beginning and continuing a relationship with Him.

The second session focused on the **benefits of being a Christian.** Your students discovered that these include salvation, forgiveness, God's protection and power, and becoming a part of His family.

Students also examined **the cost of discipleship**, and learned that being a follower of Christ requires not only a one-time decision, but a continuing willingness to submit to the Lord's control.

Then students took a look at **Bible study**, at the importance of God's Word and its value to the Christian's life. One session dealt with some of the difficulties students have in reading God's Word, and suggested tools, such as an easy-to-read version, a Bible concordance, or a dictionary, that may be used to make Bible study more profitable.

The session on **prayer** emphasized being able to pray anywhere, at any time, to a God who hears our prayers and who is interested in us.

Next your students examined the **Church**, which is the family of God's people; they looked at what the Church is to do for them, and at their responsibilities to the Church.

Developing a **Christlike life-style** was the next topic; students examined attributes of Christ and discussed how these could be demonstrated in their relationships with others.

This was followed by a study of **love**, which is the essence of the Christian life-style. Love is not just an emotion, but is demonstrated by actions taken for the benefit of the loved person.

Friendship was the next topic, with a stress on the importance of developing relationships with people of good character, and developing good character in oneself.

The final session focused on **the world's influences** and how Christians can prevent their minds from being diverted from the values that Christ taught to the values of the world.

The studies completed during this course should give your students a good understanding of the basics of Christian living.

Students who have not yet received Christ may find that this review of the course helps

them gain a new perspective of the issues of Christianity. They may need some encouragement from you to help them make a decision. Meet with them individually before or after class, or make arrangements to get together during the week.

SESSION PLAN

Attention Grabber

ATTENTION GRABBER (3-5 minutes)

Locate the "Man on the Street" section of your Treasure Seeker worksheet. Read the questions and answer them by filling in the empty balloons. Keep in mind our past sessions on the Christian life.

Allow students to work for a few moments. Then ask for volunteers to share answers. Review briefly, using material from INSIGHTS FOR THE LEADER sections of the preceding sessions.

Bible Exploration

EXPLORATION (20-30 minutes)

Step 1 (15-20 minutes): Say to your class, **Take a look at the crossword puzzle. Work in teams of three to look up the Scripture and fill in the correct words in the puzzle. You will have 20 minutes to work. When you have finished, bring your puzzle to me and I'll check your answers.**

Allow students to work. As teams bring their puzzles for checking, mark any wrong answers and

let them try again. When teams finish early, give them a copy of the "Quiz Questions" and let them work together to figure out the answers.

Step 2 (5-10 minutes): When time is up (or when all teams have finished) comment on the concepts found in the puzzle, using information from previous sessions.

Conclusion and Decision

CONCLUSION (3-5 minutes)

Conclude the session by saying, **Turn to the "Lookin' Back" graph on your Treasure Seeker. During the last three months you have probably grown in many areas. Please fill out the graph, showing areas in which you feel you have grown. Do not compare yourself to anyone else. Concentrate on graphing your own growth.**

Allow students to complete the assignment.

Close in prayer, thanking God for the growth students have experienced during this course and expressing trust in His ability to help them continue to grow.

Distribute the Fun Page as students leave.

Answers to "Quiz Questions" student worksheet activity:

1. From 22 to 28 times.
2. Red.
3. Usually on the left. (On the right in Mexico.)
4. To the left.
5. Vertical.
6. One white key.

Man on the Street

Fill in the cartoon balloons with appropriate responses.

EXCUSE ME— COULD YOU TELL ME WHAT "BELIEVE" MEANS TO YOU?

WHAT ARE SOME **BENEFITS** OF BEING A CHRISTIAN?

HOW DOES A CHRISTIAN GROW?

SORRY FOR THE **HOLD UP,** BUT WHAT **RESPONSIBILITIES** DO CHRISTIANS HAVE FOR OTHERS?

ACME BANK

TELLER

ACROSS

1. According to John 1:12, what must we do to become a child of God?
3. When we confess our sins, God _____ us. (1 John 1:9)
4. We must _____ or walk in Christ if we are to grow. (Col. 2:6)
5. Jesus tells us that if we are to follow Him we must _____ ourselves. (Luke 9:23.)
7. (Along with 10 down and 8 down.) We should pray because "everyone who _____ receives; he who finds; and to him who _____, the door will be opened." (Matt 7:8.)
9. (Along with 6 down.) Romans 12:2 warns us not to be _____ (6 down) to the pattern of the world, but to be _____ (9 across) by the renewing of your mind.
11. Another benefit given to us as Christians is _____ from the Holy Spirit (Col. 1:10,11.)
12. _____ comes from hearing the message. (Romans 10:17.)
15. The Bible is a tool in God's hand. It is "like a hammer which shatters a rock" (Jer. 23:29, NASB.) What is it like to a new baby Christian? Spiritual _____. (See 1 Pet. 2:2.)
17. Jesus says we must always _____. (Luke 18:1.)
19. Christians are commanded to _____ one another. (John 13:34.)
21. "Bad _____ corrupts good character." (1 Cor. 15:33.)
22. A Bible concordance is one _____ that is very helpful in finding Scripture dealing with a particular word.
23. His divine power has given us _____ we need for life and godliness (2 Pet 1:3)

DOWN

1. Galatians 6:2 says, "Carry each other's _____."
2. As obedient Christians, we are to prepare our minds for action and to be self-controlled; and we are not to conform to _____ desires. (1 Pet. 1:13,14.)
3. Bible study and memory are important tools in growing as a Christian. What else do we need?
6. See 9 across.
8. See 7 across.
10. See 7 across.
13. Philippians 2:7 says Christ took the very nature of a _____ and that our attitudes should be humble in the same way.
14. As God's children we are to _____ Him. (Eph. 5:1.)
16. John 3:16 says that those who believe in Christ shall have eternal _____
18. Christians are part of a _____ and should build one another up. (Gal. 6:10.)
20. To show our love to Jesus we must _____. (See John 14:15.)

Quiz Questions

1. How many times does the numeral one (1) or the word (one) appear on a U.S. one-dollar bill? Serial numbers don't count.
2. Which light, green or red, appears on top of a traffic signal?
3. On which side of the sink is the hot water tap usually found?
4. Which way does the eagle's head face on a U.S. quarter?
5. Are the buttonholes of a man's shirt vertical or horizontal?
6. Does the keyboard of a piano begin with one or two white keys?

Lookin' Back

Sometimes it does us good to stop and evaluate how our life has been going.

The graph below will help you figure out which areas of growing as a Christian you are doing well in, and which areas need improvement.

Try to be honest. (You don't need to compare with anyone.) So, graph out how you have grown in each of these areas IN THE LAST 3 MONTHS; how you're doing now as opposed to 3 months ago.

	not so hot	once in a while	working at it	most of the time	GREAT!
Gaining knowledge of Scripture					
Having friends of good character					
Winning people to Christ by your example					
Regular Bible study					
Prayer					
Love					

BATTING A THOUSAND!

If you want to take a swing at being a major league Christian (one who is mature and growing), step up to the batter's box and knock in a few runs. Here's how: Get two coins (pennies are best). Place one penny on the "Batter's Box" below. Using the other coin as a bat—as shown in the drawing—hit the penny toward any one of the baseball mitts. If the penny touches a mitt, you score 10 points. If not, subtract two points from your score. The game is ended when you have hit all mitts. You can play this game alone or with a friend. To make it tougher, close your eyes when at bat, or try to hit all 12 mitts just one time each.

BELIEVE IN GOD

"For God so loved the world that he gave his one and only Son, that whoever believes in him shall not perish but have eternal life."
John 3:16

DO WHAT GOD SAYS

"Why do you call me, 'Lord, Lord,' and do not do what I say?"
Luke 6:46

USE THE BIBLE

"Do your best to present yourself to God as one approved, a workman who does not need to be ashamed and who correctly handles the word of truth."
2 Timothy 2:15

REMEMBER THE BENEFITS

"I pray . . . that you may know the hope to which he has called you, the riches of his glorious inheritance in the saints, and his incomparably great power for us who believe."
Ephesians 1:18,19

LIVE FOR THE LORD

"So then, just as you received Christ Jesus as Lord, continue to live in him."
Colossians 2:6

READ THE BIBLE

"Consequently, faith comes from hearing the message, and the message is heard through the word of Christ."
Romans 10:17

TALK TO GOD

"Pray continually."
1 Thessalonians 5:17

DO GOOD

"Let us do good to all people, especially to those who belong to the family of believers."
Galatians 6:10

Remember: If you want to bat a thousand in your Christian life, practice the advice in these Bible verses!

BE LIKE JESUS

"Be imitators of God, therefore, as dearly loved children."
Ephesians 5:1

SHOW LOVE

"All men will know that you are my disciples, if you love one another."
John 13:35

DON'T LET THE WORLD WIPE YOU OUT

CHOOSE CHRISTIAN FRIENDS

"Do two walk together unless they have agreed to do so?"
Amos 3:3

"Do not conform any longer to the pattern of this world, but be transformed by the renewing of your mind."
Romans 12:2

DAILY NUGGETS

Day 1	Read John 1:12. Have you received Him and become a child of God? If not, what's holding you back?
Day 2	1 Corinthians 10:13. When you are tempted to do wrong, try repeating this verse.
Day 3	John 14:15. Are you showing your love for Jesus by keeping His commandments?
Day 4	Hebrews 4:12. What has the Word been doing in your life lately?
Day 5	2 Corinthians 8:9. What are some of the riches you have because of Jesus' poverty?
Day 6	2 Peter 1:3. What are some of the provisions for "life and godliness" that you have experienced?

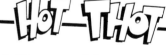

"I have hidden your word in my heart that I might not sin against you."

Psalm 119:11

Batter's Box

THE COMPLETE JUNIOR HIGH BIBLE STUDY RESOURCE BOOK #1
© 1987 GL/LIGHT FORCE, VENTURA, CA 93006

THEME: A habit of prayer, Bible study, fellowship, faith, commitment, confession, and thankfulness will make a believer very strong.

BIBLE STUDY OUTLINE

Tell students you only have one verse to cover with them: **Colossians 2:6. As time permits, make these important points:**

- If you have received Christ, you have received Him as Lord. He is your guide, master, boss. You are to obey and follow Him. You are to be like Him.
- And you are, the Bible says, to continue to live in Him. Not just once a week or when it's convenient. Not just for a few months until the fun wears off. You are to be His always.
- You are to be rooted in Him. A tree stands strong because of its roots. Many trees are just as large underground as above. Being rooted in Christ will allow you to be "built up in Him."
- The basic things you need to do to develop these roots and this maturity are: prayer, Bible study and memorization, fellowship, faith, commitment, and confession of sin.
- **Prayer** means conversing *with* God, not just asking Him for favors. Your prayer time is the time you get to know God as a friend.
- Plan a short time each day when you will **read and meditate on a passage of Scripture**. The Gospel of Mark is a good place to start.
- **Be involved in our group.** Not just as a "bench warmer," but as someone who can be counted on to help make our meetings and events good ones.
- **Faith** is an attitude of dependence on God. Trust Him and look to Him for love and guidance.
- **Commitment** is something that so many people seem to lack. It means that you should allow God to radically change your life for the better.
- **Confession of sin** allows you to remain on the cutting edge of usefulness to God and to our group.
- Finally, the Bible speaks of overflowing with **joy**. This is the sort of attitude you will experience when you have centered your life on Christ by making a habit of all these things.

OBJECT LESSON:
THE STRENGTH OF MANY STRANDS

Materials needed: A spool of thread and scissors.

Before the session, practice this lesson to determine how many loops of thread it will take to make an unbreakable trap.

As you begin to compare making a habit of prayer, Bible reading and the rest to making an unbreakable rope from many strands, ask for a volunteer to assist you. Loop the thread around his wrists one time and ask him to try to break free. He'll be able to do so easily. Then wrap the thread two or three times and ask him to break free. Even though it takes more effort, he should be able to break the thread.

Now loop the thread 15 or 20 times around his wrists. As you loop, talk about the various activities a Christian should be doing to become strong and mature. Point out that when a person is making a habit of prayer, fellowship, study and the rest, he or she is building an unbreakable rope that will bind him or her to the proper Christian life and to God.

Ask the volunteer to break free. When he can't, say, **My point exactly! Reading the Bible once a year isn't going to help you much. But make all of these things we've been talking about a habit, and your Christian life will be strong and unbreakable.**

Use the scissors to cut the person loose.

DISCUSSION QUESTIONS

1. **What does the word "Lord" mean? Why might it be hard for someone living in this country to understand the idea of a Lord?**
2. **What are the advantages of having Jesus as Lord?**
3. **Is it sometimes hard for people your age to act as if Jesus is Lord? If so, why? What are some of the reasons?**
4. **Do you think it's as hard for older Christians to act as if Jesus is Lord? Why or why not?**
5. **What can we do together and as individuals to make it easier to live for God?**

THE COMPLETE JUNIOR HIGH
BIBLE STUDY RESOURCE
BOOK #1

Welcome to the boxing matches.

"ALL BOXED IN"

A typical relay race. The catch here is that contestants must "run" the race with both feet in a strong corrugated cardboard box. Keep a couple of spare boxes on hand just in case.

VARIATION:

Allow players to run on all fours with a box on each hand and foot. Great on a slippery rug.

"BOX CAR RACES"

Another relay race. This one is for as many teams as you can form of eight to ten players each. Each team elects two or three players to push a cardboard box across the course, which must be a rug. Another player stands in the box as it is pushed. If the player falls, he or she must get back in the box. The race continues until all participants (except the pushers) have had a chance to ride the boxes.

"A BOX OF LAFFS"

If you have a large appliance box or two, see how many kids can be packed inside. Have the box open at both ends for safety.

"Bible Wars" OPTIONAL SESSION

This alternate session plan represents a departure from the usual format of this course. It gives students a change of pace and a welcome "breather." At the same time, it provides a review (or a preview) of Bible truths covered in the course.

Begin by explaining the rules of "Bible Wars" (as found below). Then have students form teams of no more than 10 to 15 members each. If you have more than 30 students, recruit another adult to help you. Have two sets of teams competing in separate rooms; then have play-offs, with losers playing losers and winners playing winners. Make sure all students are assigned to teams and given an opportunity to play.

If you have an odd number of students, so that the teams are unequal, one member of the smaller team gets "two lives" (that is, he or she will not be eliminated the first time someone attempts to put him or her "out," as explained in the rules that follow). Select this student at random with a gimmick such as, "The person whose birthday is closest to February 4."

SPECIAL PREVIEW / REVIEW SESSION

HOW TO PLAY "BIBLE WARS"

After all students have been assigned to teams, have them arrange their chairs so that each team sits in a row of chairs facing the other team. Also designate a "spectators' section" that can be monitored easily; when students are declared "out" of the game, they will sit in this section.

Now find the "Scripture Verses for 'Bible Wars' " sheet. Begin the game by calling out the first Scripture reference. Students are to find the Scripture in their Bible and jump to their feet. The first person to jump up and start reading the correct verse is the winner of the round. Everyone else must sit down while this person continues to read the verse. Anyone who can quote the verse correctly from memory without looking it up in the Bible may do so.

If the person reads or quotes the verse correctly, he or she may eliminate any student from the opposite team. The eliminated student must remain "out" for the rest of the game and cannot help his or her team in any way except to cheer and encourage them. Students who are "out" may not harass the other team. There is to be no trading places: the student chosen to go "out" must go "out."

If the person first on his or her feet reads or quotes the wrong verse, he or she "self-destructs" and goes out. Play will continue with a new verse. (Accept a verse quoted from memory if it is reasonably accurate.)

The game continues until one team is eliminated completely (or until you run out of time).

If you wish, you may use a "bonus question" with every fifth Scripture that is read or quoted correctly. Bonus questions are found at the bottom of the Scripture verses sheet. Students who correctly answer a bonus question get a "second life"; in other words, they cannot be eliminated the first time someone calls them "out"; it takes two such calls before they go "out." This also applies to students who "self-destruct"; if they have a "second life," they do not go out after their first incorrect answer. (If you are using this session before the end of the course, do not use the bonus questions, as students will not have studied the lessons and will have a hard time answering; or use only those questions relating to sessions already covered. There are two questions per session and they are in the same order as the sessions.)

Bibles with tabs or thumb indexes are not allowed.

Scripture verses for "Bible Wars"

John 1:12	Psalm 103:12	1 John 5:2	Luke 6:12	2 Corinthians 2:14	John 14:31	Proverbs 18:24
John 7:38	2 Timothy 1:7	Ephesians 4:13	Romans 10:17	1 Corinthians 5:1-7	Mark 6:34	Romans 13:12
John 3:23	Ephesians 6:11	1 Thessalonians 5:17	2 Timothy 3:16	Ephesians 5:1	2 Corinthians 8:9	1 John 2:15
Acts 16:30	1 John 1:9	1 John 5:14	1 Peter 2:2	Luke 7:11	Romans 5:8	1 Peter 1:13
John 6:40	Colossians 2:6,7	Matthew 7:7	Jeremiah 23:29	Galatians 5:22,23	Philippians 2:5	Genesis 39:11,12
John 3:16	2 Timothy 2:15	James 1:5	Hebrews 4:2	1 John 3:16	Galatians 6:10	James 4:4
John 11:25	Psalm 119:11	Daniel 6:10	John 20:31	John 13:34	Hebrews 10:24	Matthew 13:22
Ephesians 1:18,19	Luke 18:1	Hebrews 4:16	Colossians 1:5	Romans 8:29	1 Thessalonians 5:11	2 Peter 1:3
John 6:47	Acts 2:42	Philippians 4:6	Psalm 119:105	Luke 23:43	Amos 3:3	Ephesians 4:22
1 Corinthians 10:13	Hebrews 8:12,13	Psalm 86:6	Romans 1:6	1 Timothy 1:16	1 Corinthians 15:33	James 4:7
Acts 1:8	Isaiah 59:1,2	Ephesians 6:18	Jeremiah 5:14	Matthew 5:14	Galatians 6:2	2 Timothy 2:22
Ephesians 2:19	Luke 6:46	Luke 5:16	Isaiah 58:11	John 15:10	Proverbs 11:13	1 John 4:1
1 Thessalonians 5:9	John 14:15	Luke 18:10	Psalm 33:20	Matthew 11:29,30	1 John 2:10	1 Peter 2:11
Romans 3:23	Mark 12:30	John 11:38	Hebrews 4:12	Mark 10:16	Proverbs 3:13,14	2 Timothy 3:2
Luke 24:49	Romans 12:2	Luke 9:16	John 6:63	Luke 21:15	2 Corinthians 6:14	
Hebrews 8:12	Matthew 10:37	Acts 9:39	Matthew 11:28	Matthew 19:14	Colossians 3:13	

1. Give a definition of the word "believe." (Trust, rely on, cling to, put your faith in.)
2. All those who believe in Christ become what to God? (His children.)
3. Name one benefit of becoming a Christian. (Any of these: salvation, protection, forgiveness, power, a family.)
4. The power of God comes to us through _____. (The Holy Spirit.)
5. Jesus said that before you put up a building (become a Christian) you should _____. (Count the cost.)
6. If we love Christ we will _____ Him. (Obey.)
7. God's desire for Christians is that they do not stay the same but that they _____. (Grow.)
8. Name one important practice that promotes Christian growth. (Any of these: prayer, Bible study, Bible memory, fellowship.)
9. Name one thing God's Word is good for. (Any of these: wisdom, teaching, instruction, reproof, equipping for righteousness.)
10. In order to know what God has to say, we have to _____. (Read His Word.)
11. Name one tool that will help you understand God's Word better. (Any of these: pencil and paper; colored pencils; Bible with cross-references; easy-to-read version; English dictionary; Bible dictionary; concordance; Bible resource person.)
12. If you read something you don't understand in God's Word, what should you do? (Write it down and ask a Bible resource person, or check Bible study tools.)
13. Prayer is _____. (Talking to God.)
14. Where can a Christian pray? (Anywhere.)
15. What is the Church? (People who have received Christ.)
16. How do you become a member of the true Church? (Receive Christ.)
17. A model for a Christian to imitate is _____. (Christ.)
18. Name one of Christ's characteristics which a Christian can imitate. (Any of these: love, compassion, humility, gentleness, obedience to God and parents, patience, forgiveness.)
19. What is the mark of a Christian? (Love.)
20. How did Christ show His love for us? (He died for us.)
21. The Bible tells us that bad friends will do what to us? (Any of these: mess us up, corrupt us, get us off the track spiritually.)
22. Name one characteristic of a good friend. (Any of these: agreement on important matters, especially spiritual things; bearing others' burdens; standing by a friend; walking in the light; forgiveness.)
23. Name one medium the world uses to communicate its messages. (Any of these: TV, radio, newspapers, magazines, books, etc.)
24. Name one thing you can do to decide which of the world's ideas are right or wrong. (Read the Bible and judge what you hear by its message.)

169

CLIP ART AND OTHER GOODIES

The following pages contain all sorts of fun, high quality clip art. Put it to good use: brighten up your youth group's mail outs, bulletins, posters, and overhead transparencies. Cut 'em out, paste 'em up, run 'em off, and there you have it!

The **Other Goodies** include our **Bible Study Chart** and **Prayer Chart,** referred to in a couple of the **Session Plans.** They will help your students focus in on two important ingredients for spiritual growth.

WANT TO PRODUCE GREAT PROMOTIONAL MATERIAL?
TURN THE PAGE FOR EASY INSTRUCTIONS.

EASY INSTRUCTIONS

1. **Get a sheet of clean white paper. This will become the master for your promotional piece.**

2. **Choose the art you want from this section. Cut it out and glue it to the master. Or use the art intended for backgrounds as your master.**

3. **Add headlines with rub-on letters (available at any art store) or with a felt pen. Add body copy with a typewriter or by hand. (Type on a separate sheet and cut and paste.)**

4. **Run off as many copies as you need, hand them out or drop them in the mail. Presto!**

TIPS:

Go heavy on the artwork, light on the copy. A piece with too many words goes unread.

Get in the habit of making a monthly calendar of events. It doesn't have to be an expensive masterpiece; just so it tells your group members what they can find at your church.

Print the calendar on the back of the **Treasure Seeker** worksheets or the **Fun Page.** This will insure that those pages are saved and reread.

MOUNTAIN MANIA

MOUNTAIN MANIA

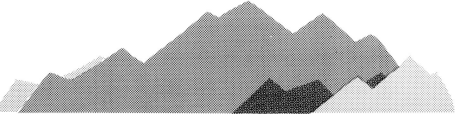

MOUNTAIN MANIA

This Month:

This Month:

This Month:

MOUNTAIN MANIA

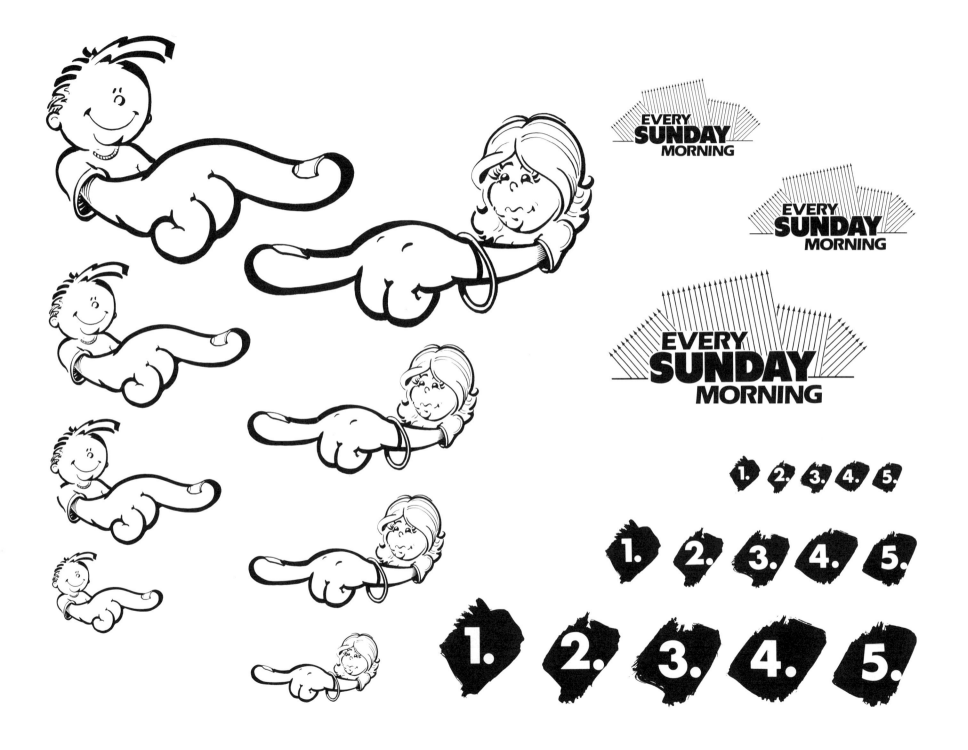

This Month:

Bible Study Chart

Keeping track of what you have read and learned can be a great help to your spiritual growth. In the "Comments" space you can record special insights, blessings, or questions you may have. If you really wish to get a lot from your Bible, use study tools such as a Bible dictionary, English dictionary, Bible concordance, and a Bible with cross-references.

DATE	PASSAGE READ	COMMENTS

PRAYER CHART

Use this chart to help you get a better grasp of who or what you pray for, things you are thankful for and God's response to your prayer.

DATE	PRAISES	REQUESTS	ANSWERS

GREAT THINGS FROM THE LIGHT FORCE!

OUTRAGEOUS OBJECT LESSONS

Your students' attention will be riveted on the truth of God's Word when you take advantage of these wonderful object lessons. Ranging from the very simple to the outrageous, from the classic to the unique, these lessons will greatly increase the retention time of your messages.

THE YOUTH WORKER'S BOOK OF CASE STUDIES

Over fifty true stories with discussion questions.

Nothing grabs a student's interest like a true story focused on the real problems and situations young people face today. Your Bible talks take on a new dimension of interest and impact when you spice them up with these terrific object lessons and true case studies.

Subjects range from abortion to gossip to self-image and beyond.

A few of the object lessons and case studies on the POPSHEETS were taken from these two resource books. If you want over one hundred great ideas to liven up your own teaching times, you'll want OUTRAGEOUS OBJECT LESSONS and CASE STUDIES!

Order now from your local Christian supplier, or call us toll free.

800-235-3415 (Outside California)   800-227-4025 (California only)

MORE CRE